Uncertain refuge

Lectures on Newfoundland society and culture

Uncertain refuge

Lectures on Newfoundland society and culture

by Maura Hanrahan, Ph.D.

Breakwater
100 Water Street
P.O. Box 2188
St. John's, Newfoundland
A1C 6E6

Canadian Cataloguing in Publication Data
Uncertain refuge
ISBN 1-55081-087-1
1. Newfoundland — Social conditions.
I. Hanrahan, Maura, 1963-
HN110.N4U63 1993 971.8'04 C93-098668-7

Design and typesetting by Wendy Smith, Toronto

This book is dedicated
with love to the memory
of Peter John Wicks,
1964-1993.

Contents

Acknowledgements ix

Introduction xi

Unit 1 The historical heritage of Newfoundland

Lecture 1	Toward an understanding of Newfoundland society and history	3
Lecture 2	Early settlement patterns in Newfoundland	10
Lecture 3	Irish migration to Newfoundland	16
Lecture 4	Class in Newfoundland society	21
Lecture 5	St. John's—Newfoundland's capital city in history	25
Lecture 6	Society and social life in St. John's	29

References for Unit 1 37

Unit 2 Grassroots politics in Newfoundland

Introduction 41

Lecture 1	Women and politics—a separate sphere?	44
Reading	*This is democracy? Reflections on the occupation experience* by T. MacKenzie	52
Lecture 2	'The protest line' in Burin—fighting government and business	56

References for Unit 2 63

Unit 3 Social conflict and problems in Newfoundland

Lecture 1	Abuse by consensus	67
Lecture 2	The concept of the family	72
Lecture 3	Family experiences through children's eyes	75
Reading	*Never despair is author's message in novel* by Nina Patey	79
Lecture 4	Women and the family in Newfoundland	84

References for Unit 3 88

Unit 4 Work and development in Newfoundland

Lecture 1	Industrialization in Newfoundland	93
Lecture 2	Resettlement in Newfoundland	100
Lecture 3	Government dependency and regional policy	108
Lecture 4	Life as an industrial worker	112
Reading	(Excerpts from) *Chapter 10: They didn't do their duty* by Elliott Leyton	119
Lecture 5	The fishing industry	123
Lecture 6	Newfoundland culture and the sealing industry	133
Lecture 7	The seal hunt protests	139
Reading	(Excerpts from) *A day on the ice* by Guy Wright	144

References for Unit 4 144

Acknowledgements

I would like to offer my sincere thanks to the following:

the Division of Continuing Studies at MUN;
the Division of Educational Technology, especially Janice Neary and her staff;
Dr. Thomas Nemec; Patrick Hanrahan; Mark Dolomount; and Andrew Boone;
the many students over the past few years who have left notes under my door or called me urging me to 'keep up the good work' and 'write a book on this stuff someday'. Here it is! I wish I could adequately impart to them how inspiring their sense of discovery is.
And, finally, Thomas Merton, who gives me calm and hope without ever knowing I exist.

Introduction

Uncertain Refuge: Lectures on Newfoundland Society and Culture is primarily a sociological exploration of issues concerning the history, polity, culture and economy of the island of Newfoundland. My purview here is from the European contacts that laid the foundation for modern-day Newfoundland society, such as the West Country migratory fishery, right up to the 1990s, a time when international economics and politics as well as the (not unrelated) depletion of the Northern Cod and other fish stocks make so many vital questions so difficult to answer. Indeed, Newfoundlanders' collective self-esteem and sense of self-sufficiency, already battered from within and without for a dangerously long time, are in further peril. Having identified my time frame and, in so doing, alluded to a smattering of current, pivotal questions, I must emphasise that this book makes no attempt to answer these questions. Nor does this book concern itself with prehistoric life in Newfoundland or the societies and cultures of Labrador: these omissions are reflections not on the worthiness of these subjects but only on my own inadequacies as a scholar. The purpose of *Uncertain Refuge* is a product singularly of the nature of those the original lectures were directed to: my students.

Uncertain Refuge—published as a companion volume to *Through a Mirror Dimly*, a collection of essays on Newfoundland society and culture—was conceived in 1990 as a central part of a university correspondence course for sociology and anthropology students who wished to investigate Newfoundland society and culture using the tools and methods offered by the social sciences. These students, the majority at the early undergraduate level, were scattered throughout the island, Labrador and beyond. I was able to design, develop and deliver the course, with these lectures as my axis, through Memorial University's Division of Continuing

Studies. This, the book that is the fruit of these lectures, is written for my students; consequently, it is written in a style that is accessible to them. It is not composed using academic language as its main vehicle and, although I am an academic, I do not apologize for that. While scholastic language is useful, necessary and even beautiful in the hands of a master, its restricted essence is also its greatest failure. Like the idiom of medical and legal practitioners, our vernacular can obscure truths waiting to be found and rob so many of knowledge and its Siamese twin, power. Throughout the history of Newfoundland (and so very many places like it) this unforgivable theft has occurred. *Uncertain Refuge* is, in part, a small attempt at restitution.

This book is not an attempt to propose solutions for Newfoundland's social and economic problems and nor is it an undertaking to teach students the forms of sociological writing. What is this book for then? Its missions are simple, but crucial and not unambitious: that is, if we are to cope successfully with any of the myriad of crises that we face presently, we must learn to think *analytically* about our society, our situation and all the factors, within and without, affecting it. That is, if we are to bring about positive social, cultural, economic or political change on either a micro or macro level, our mind set must shift dramatically. The same applies if we are to keep what is worth preserving. For this to happen either now or at some glorious time in the future, critical thinking is necessary and this includes self-criticism or review and reprieval of the failings and defects of Newfoundland as a culture, then and now.

As a teacher and as the author of *Uncertain Refuge,* I want to do nothing less than at least try to change the way we as Newfoundlanders construct our identity and culture and think about ourselves. Progress of any sort requires an abandonment of notions of victimization (whether real or socially constructed, it does not matter) and a commitment to a fresh, constructive manner of seeing ourselves and our place in the wider world.

This ominous task requires a debunking of many of the myths that are imprinted in our minds and in the minds of others as facts. These are innumerable and they serve as barriers to social and cultural growth. One of these falsities is that Newfoundland is a set of black and white, and then colour, pictures rather than a panoramic moving film. In other words, we often conceive of our history as a collection of completely separate and autonomous time periods and concomitant lifestyles; as it is most commonly put, there were 'the old days' and 'the modern times'. Occasionally this faulty vision of Newfoundland history is articulated as pre-Confederation and post-Confederation: sometimes it is not. Either way, it is a damaging simplification of the way most societies, including Newfoundland, really function. Another frustrating case is the exceedingly popular cultural presentation of Newfoundlanders as jolly, quaint, dialect-ridden 'Newfies', good for a laugh but not especially hard-working or skilled at anything. This stereotype, equivalent to the southern black 'mammy' or the smelly, dirty 'Paki' is perpetuated within the province as well as from outside. 'Newfie' has become in our minds a representation of this culture but its image is hardly an accurate one. In addition, it is a simplification of a society and culture that is just as complex and complicated as any other in the modern world, but that point is so easily overlooked. In Newfoundland, as elsewhere, social change, propelled by internal or external forces or the interplay between them, is the only constant.

The everpresence of change in a society does not cancel out the strong element of persistence that exists in most societies. In examining Newfoundland society we have tended to stress the theme of persistence, or continuity: witness, for example, the recurrence through the centuries of folksongs about the formidableness of the sea. Another illustration of persistence is the continuing significance of the fisheries to cultural, economic and political life here. In recent years sociologists and anthropologists have focused on the perseverative theme of occupational pluralism in Newfoundland life; that is, due to our particular amalgam of geography and ecology there has always been a need to combine a number of economic activities, such as hunting, fishing and farming, to eke out a living. This reality is recognized and referred to throughout *Uncertain Refuge*. There are other lesser celebrated elements to which the reader is asked to direct his or her attention. For instance, women in Newfoundland, like women elsewhere, have never enjoyed the status, recognition and rewards that their brothers, fathers and husbands have, no matter what sort of economic, cultural or social enterprise we may look at. And despite the constant social change that I have said figures so prominently in our history, the status of women has remained consistently lower than that of men. This is evident in cultural manifestations like popular Newfoundland songs as well as in, say, employment and property legislation that has squarely identified women as less meritorious than men. The theme of continuing, if hidden, abuse is also an important one in Newfoundland society although it has only recently become a public focus of the media, the justice system and, of course, some of the multitude of victims that walk through life. A competent social scientist learns that things are rarely as they seem; a stunningly beautiful outport setting can be a concentration camp for children, women, the ill, the elderly and others devoid of power and influence, even over their own bodies. One of the aims of *Uncertain Refuge* is to convey the value of asking questions, even, especially, about that which we always took for granted in our society: questions about status, gender, hierarchies, traditions, rituals, roles, expectations, needs and wants, all we see around us. Persistence, like change, is not necessarily a good thing.

Some years ago a friend of mine wondered aloud at my choice to study sociology at the graduate level, reiterating that this particular academic discipline was "just a statement of the obvious". In that immediate situation I felt rattled and couldn't help but agreeing with him, staying silent about the child of Durkheim, Marx, Hegel, Weber, Mannheim, Parsons, Marcuse and the countless others (some unacknowledged) who had made contributions from anthropology, psychology, history, political science, women's studies and even medicine and religion. I sat there, quite stunned, while their stern and disappointed faces frowned at me. But my friend had given me a lot to think about. I had, in fact, wandered rather blindly into sociology: like so much else in life I'd kind of stumbled into it as the months rolled into years and my primary energies had poured into daily, instead of long-term, tasks. Being jolted out of my sense of academic shock proved useful and even liberating for me. Sociology, like the other social sciences, is, I suppose, in part at least, a statement of the obvious but it is not *merely* that.

I can honestly say that sociology has changed and immeasurably improved my life: I am not referring to education in general when I say this but to the scope and the uniqueness of this discipline. It has provided me with the tools to see the ordinary in a different, liberating way: the ordinary being the things that surround us, the things we take for granted, the things that may choke our development as individuals and as societies. I do not believe that objectivity is ever possible. There is too much of society and socialization in us, as individuals, for us to be completely unbiased: once we choose a subject to write about or draw, for example, we have lost whatever there might have been of objectivity. Perhaps the computer I am writing this on is capable of detachment but a social and socialized being is not. Having said this, I maintain that sociology has afforded me new ways of seeing, fresh eyes if you like, almost like eyes that are only seeing aspects of society and culture for the first time (the proverbial alien who just landed from Mars). Put simply, studying society in a systematic way has allowed me as one person to take what I like and leave the rest in constructing a life that will be fulfilling for me. By identifying what is society at work versus what are my own views, desires or needs, I am freed, if I so choose to be. One can act in this way and live within society. One can also work for change or strive to preserve what ought to be kept. I remember an aging professor telling his cynical, semi-interested students "knowledge is beautiful but it hurts". Knowledge brings a glorious pain and with its presence you know you are alive.

Any student knows that knowledge can be elusive. Through reading *Uncertain Refuge* I hope that you achieve some proficiency in the use of the tools of sociological analysis while examining Newfoundland society and culture. As sociologists we take nothing for granted, as I've implied. We attempt to identify patterns: did economic power generally mean that social control accrued to the outport merchants? did women's involvement in political struggles usually lead to victory? Sociologists try to zero in on the roles institutions, for instance, play, irrespective of the roles they claim to play: does the family provide a safe haven for most women and children? does government provide financial assistance for mining and fishing corporations because it wishes to ensure the gainful employment of its citizens? Sociologists endeavour to dissect rituals or rites of passage: what was the cultural meaning of the Blessing of the Fleet? what purpose did this ceremony serve? what are the social and economic purposes of marriage as played out in wedding traditions? Sociologists undertake to delineate the social and economic hierarchies that societies build: which institutions facilitate the oppression of certain groups in society? which institutions assist in our advantageous development? which rituals suppress individuality?

which processes enable groups and individuals to evolve rather than evaporate?

Uncertain Refuge aims to present you with moving pictures of Newfoundland society and culture. Unfortunately, I fear I have come up short somewhat in my effort to refrain from providing answers. Consequently, I urge you to bear in mind that the lectures that follow constitute the views of only one sociologist. They are by no means *correct*. The concept of correctness, like objectivity, is a non-entity, although there are great pressures from lobby groups, ideologues in and outside of universities, and various quarters of the media to make it a primary consideration in a socio-cultural discourse of this type. Correctness is as stifling as much of what it professes to oppose, isolating for many, and quite often a substitute for original thought. In research papers and in class, I encourage my students to disagree with whatever positions surface, if they so choose, as long as their dissention is not kneejerk, but borne of thought and deliberation and buttressed by evidence. There is enormous fun to be had by argument. Besides, sociology is a pluralistic field. It is active debate in academia that makes the whole exercise healthy and productive: torpor benefits no one.

I also beseech the reader to be aware that while *Uncertain Refuge* is wide-ranging in the topics it touches on, it cannot be complete with respect to Newfoundland society and culture. Due to a number of limitations, including, for instance, time and space, there are a number of subjects prominently absent: education, religion, crime and justice are among them. Still, I hope that this glimpse at Newfoundland's heritage, grassroots politics, social problems, and issues of work and development will contribute in some small way to your enjoyment of this wonderful, troubled place and to new and rewarding ways of thinking about it.

What follows is a glossary of basic sociological concepts designed to orient you to the systematic, critical study of Newfoundland society and culture. These terms are used universally by social scientists and, therefore, an understanding of them will enable you to develop a foundation for further studies in the social sciences.

Maura Catherine Hanrahan
April, 1993

Unit One

The historical heritage of Newfoundland

Lecture 1

Toward an understanding of Newfoundland society and history

You may have heard it said that to understand our history is to understand ourselves. Certainly, while contemporary institutions influence us, those of our past played an important part in our becoming who we are. Very often a close examination of a society's past can help explain its present features. For example, many tourists visiting Newfoundland often inquire as to why this province's settlements are so "strung out" along a very long coastline. Sometimes the emptiness (people-wise) of the interior of the island baffles people, particularly if they are from inland towns or cities, like those on the Canadian prairies. There are a number of factors that account for our sparse settlement pattern here in Newfoundland and we can look to our history to uncover them. The English and Irish fishermen who fished our summer waters were prohibited from establishing permanent homes here because the British feared losing control of the fishery. This is one reason why there are communities tucked away in so many unexpected places in Newfoundland. The traditional importance of the fishing industry (our *raison d'être,* in fact) explains why our ancestors flocked to the coast and set up homes there (as opposed to the interior). This is just one simple example of how our historical heritage has contributed to our identity, lifestyle and culture.

This treatise does not cover the island's *prehistory*: the history for which we have little written record and must rely upon archaeological evidence (such as the remains of the Viking settlement at L'Anse aux Meadows on the Great Northern Peninsula). The reason for this omission is that our prehistory has played a very limited part in constructing our present-day society. The Beothuck Indians, as you know, all died out by the early part of the 1800s. It's true that this fact and the myths and truths surrounding it and other aspects of our prehistory have had some effect, perhaps on our attitudes about ourselves for instance, but in the main these are minimal. The situation differs drastically for Labrador where aboriginal peoples make up a significant part of modern society but Newfoundland is largely, *almost* exclusively, comprised of the descendants of Europeans.

In a fifteenth century letter Raimonds di Somsino wrote that: "...the sea there (around Newfoundland) is swarming with fish, which can be taken not only with the net but in baskets let down with a stone, so that it sinks in the water."[1] It was this abundant resource that attracted Europeans to our coasts; year after year, the Portuguese, Spanish, Basque, French and English successfully exploited Newfoundland's or Terra Nova's fisheries. They viewed the island as a great ship moored conveniently near the Grand Banks, rather than the supplier of natural resources itself. Throughout Newfoundland's history, our orientation has indeed been to the sea, not to the vast interior. Towns like Buchans and Grand Falls, which exploit inland resources, are relatively new in Newfoundland's history.

The importance of the fishing industry to Newfoundland society and culture is something that we often refer to, both in academic publications and in everyday conversations. And certainly prior to the northern cod moratorium imposed in 1992, the modern day fishery was one of our most significant employer; over 20,000 people were laid off when the federal government banned fishing. However, it is interesting to examine what role the industry played in the *formation* of Newfoundland society and culture. We will see that the fishery is our *raison d'être* and that it has been a

---

1 Letter to the Duke of Milan, December 18, 1497, p. 17, in Hanrahan, 1989.

crucial factor in shaping our social and cultural institutions for several centuries. One of these institutions is government: the following lecture will show how the nature of the fishing industry and resource played a vital role in the history of government in Newfoundland.

The beginnings of government on the island

The history of government in Newfoundland is unique among the former colonies of the British Empire, upon which, it has been said, the sun never sets. When we think of terms like 'imperialism' and 'colonialism' very often we imagine a foreign people taking over, usually by force, and governing a native or original people. Alternatively we picture settlers from Europe, pioneers of one sort or another, leaving home and establishing themselves in an overseas colony. Usually they are governed from the mother country (e.g., London ruled New England in its early years) and supported from there. According to Marxist analyses, wealth, in the form of fish or sugar, say, is appropriated from the colony by the imperialists and utilized for the good of the merchant classes in the imperialist country.

In many ways, Newfoundland was treated as any other colony of a European imperialist nation. For example, the island's wealth, in the form of natural resources like fish, was *expropriated* or removed for the greater good of the imperialist power. In the terminology of development theorists, the empire or colonial power *appropriates* that which creates value in the colony. The colony, in turn, does not have the economic wherewithal to prosper. Development theorists (Andre Gunder Frank, Peter Evans) view places like Newfoundland in this situation as *hinterlands,* generating profits for the larger, more powerful metropolis, such as England. (This is an idea we'll come back to in lectures on work and development.) Frank and Evans would see this relationship as an exploitive one. Similar sentiments are echoed by Newfoundland nationalists who claim that the "colonizers, England and now Canada", extract valuable resources or, to put it more bluntly, bleed or rape Newfoundland into a position of economic peril. And similar analyses are put forward relating to scores of countries and regions. In the historical case of England and Newfoundland, it's fair to say that, as with other colonies, the relationship was imbalanced in this way rather than symbiotic. In my opinion nationalist views are both too simplistic and go too far. Other, not directly economic, factors to take into account while considering the question are England's military needs, for example. We know that it was crucial in that time period to have well-trained naval officers and sailors and that Newfoundland's ability to develop these was a critical part of the island's attraction. (This is a subject of further discussion in the next lecture.)

Eventually the ties between the colony and the 'mother country' are loosened or even broken through rebellion, revolution, a variety of economic developments, war itself or other scenarios. The break between the two may be complete or it may be merely transformed; for example, the majority of the former British colonies are active in an international political organization called the Commonwealth, headed by the British monarch. Canada (and therefore Newfoundland) belongs to this agency and is considered to be one of its leaders. By appearances it is as if the often exploitive relationship that existed in the colonial period had never happened. Yet the history of one colony, Newfoundland, and in particular its history vis-à-vis Britain, has been conflict-ridden and unpredictable to say the least. As we have already said, Newfoundland's history as a colony is unique and we will look at this in some detail; in the words of the late historian Keith Matthews, "(Newfoundland) was not to be a colony like the others."[2]

We know that the earliest colonies, such as those established by John Guy in Cupids and Lord Baltimore in Ferryland, failed in the sense that the private companies that governed them could not turn profits (nor could the other colonies, e.g., Virginia) but also because

---

2 Matthews, 1988, p. 76.
The majority of the material that we will use in the rest of the Unit 1 lectures is adapted from *Lectures on the History of Newfoundland, 1500-1830*, Keith Matthews, Breakwater, St. John's, 1988. In particular we will focus on Chapters XII and XVIII: "The Development of British Policy Towards Newfoundland: Should Newfoundland be a Colony Like the Others?" and "The Expansion of Newfoundland: 1713–1775".

permanent settlement of any sort was not their end result. The King of England had given 'proprietary grants' to men like Guy as outright gifts. The proprietor of a colony was "not really answerable to anyone and could do as he pleased".[3] Yet Guy's colony, largely dependent on agriculture, did not prosper. With its small population base (much smaller than that of Virginia, for instance), Newfoundland was unable to support private firms in their quest for profit. Only the skilled fishermen, scattered throughout the island, could survive and support themselves.

Obviously, as these private colonies met their demise, so did the form of private government they had upheld. Consequently, the 'Crown Colony' was introduced in 1624: with this system, Newfoundland was controlled directly by the English Crown with no private interests in between. Even with this structure in place, the Crown found itself in a quandary vis-à-vis Newfoundland. The colony had a 'special nature', in that, unlike other colonies, it was not valued for itself but for the fish stocks that surrounded it in abundance. The crucial question became then, what form of government and settlement would best preserve the fishery for the use of the English Crown? There were two possibilities uppermost in the minds of the decision-makers:

1. to encourage the continuation and possible expansion of the migratory fishermen who came from English ports every year; or
2. to establish a permanently settled colony made up of fishermen and others.

Between 1610 and 1700, a variety of forms of government (including no government at all!) were tried in Newfoundland because the British government could not decide which one would best serve their purposes. Not surprisingly, throughout this period, the Western Adventurers wanted the settlers removed, fearing they would take the place of the migratory fishery. In the back of their minds lurked the thought that with permanent settlement and government, Newfoundland would become as independent-minded and troublesome as New England. Opposing the Western

---

[3] Matthews, p. 71.

Adventurers and their supporters were those with the view that the settlers were crucial to the fishery; without the presence of settlers the French would undoubtedly assume control of the island. The English would be barred out completely if they lost their dry fishery on land. Settlement was banned in 1675 but then permitted in 1677, albeit with much trepidation and reluctance on the part of the British.

With settlers accepted on Newfoundland soil, another decision had to be made: how should these settlers be governed? One problem was that, historically, the English government never paid the cost of colonial government. Besides, even if it had wanted to, England was poverty-stricken at that time and could not afford to fund a Newfoundland government. Another argument against the establishment of colonial powers was that the presence of organized government would encourage large numbers of immigrants to colonize the island. This, of course, would destroy the migratory fishery and this was something the Crown wanted to avoid if at all possible. In the years following, the English vacillated continually on the issue, never wholly endorsing one side or the other. Matthews assumes that they reasoned that just because settlers were necessary, government might not be necessary, especially if the island remained so sparsely populated. In fact, all that was needed was enough settlers to allow the English Crown to have some sort of legal claim to sovereignty. Despite years of inaction and indecisiveness the problem did not go away and in 1699 a compromise was reached; in that year a law, King William's Act, was passed recognizing the need for settlement in Newfoundland but rejecting the establishment of a government on the island. This solution was, as Matthews points out, unique in the British Empire.

Newfoundland was indeed, then, a colony not like the others, at least for a time. We know that her political circumstances changed several times; Newfoundland won Responsible Government in 1855; this collapsed. A Commission of Government ruled from 1933 to 1949 when we became Canada's tenth province following two referenda the year before. One of the phenomenon that we can gleam out of this cursory look at early Newfoundland is that geography, economics and culture were factors that became interwoven into what would become Newfoundland's political destiny. Taking a sociological look at early settlement in Newfoundland encompasses an interdisciplinary examination of all these characteristics and issues. As you study the factors that shaped our early history, consider how they shaped our culture and society as well, and what, if any, reverberations modern Newfoundland feels from the conflict-ridden unpredictability of a few short centuries ago.

Sociological and other terms

Appropriate [verb]—to take for oneself. E.g., some scholars contend that Central Canadian capitalist interests appropriate surplus value from the marginal or peripheral areas of the country.

Expropriate [verb]—to take from its rightful owner.

Hinterland—an area that is geographically, economically and politically removed from the decision-makers at the core (central area).

Prehistory—history that precedes written record and relies upon archaeological area.

Crown Colony—a political entity ruled directly by the Crown or Monarch with no private interests in between.

Lecture 2

Early settlement patterns in Newfoundland

Immigration

For several decades in the 18th century settlement on the island of Newfoundland was banned. This is one of the historical elements that contributes to the uniqueness of Newfoundland society. We will return to this particular subject in much more detail later in the lecture. First, though, I want to make some comments about general, less time-specific migration to the island.

One of the myths I'd like to help dispel concerns the ethnicity of the people who finally settled in Newfoundland's coves, bays and towns. We tend to think of ourselves as descendants of the English (specifically those from the West Country, counties Devon and Dorset) or the Irish (primarily counties Waterford and Wexford in southeastern Ireland). This belief is true to a large extent; it is estimated that over 95% of Newfoundlanders are of either Irish or British stock. However, we are more culturally diversified in our roots and less homogenous than we think. That is to say, besides our English and Irish influences, there are a number of others. These include: Scottish (such as in the Codroy Valley in particular); Micmac Indian (besides the Conne River Reservation, there are Micmacs in the Central Newfoundland and Stephenville areas); French (Port-au-Port Peninsula which has a culturally strong francophone community); Chinese (mostly St. John's, since early in this century); and Jewish people (again, mostly in St. John's but they became first peddlars then important merchants throughout the island).[4] More recently a variety of European and Asian people have settled all over the province, many working as professionals. The influx of Bulgarian refugees into Newfoundland in the late 1980s is already starting to leave its mark on our culture—a Bulgarian artist designed a monument to St. Lawrence and Lawn miners and the shipwrecked U.S. sailors they rescued in the 1940s, for example. Newfoundland occupies a strategic position between North America and Europe. Historically, the island has had significant and ongoing contact with the Maritimes, New England, the Caribbean, Spain, Portugal, and Britain and Ireland. So it is not surprising that such a mélange of cultures has assimilated into or at least influenced Newfoundland society.

While it might not be the case for our most recent immigrants (including say, the Chinese, the Jews and the Bulgarians), historically most people moving to the island were motivated by the presence of such rich fishing grounds. As Memorial University anthropologist Dr. Thomas Nemec has researched, the migratory (summer) fishery was strategically important to England for three reasons:

1. **As a source of employment** for thousands of West Country (Devon and Dorset) fishermen and trades people;
2. **As a revenue generator**. The English sold their saltfish to Spain, Portugal and Italy for gold and other commodities; and
3. **As a training ground for naval personnel**. Some analysts, including Nemec, feel that this was the most important factor from England's point of view.

Early settlement patterns

These first "colonies" constitute the beginning of European social and economic development on the island of Newfoundland.

---

4 You are referred to *Listen While I Tell You: The Story of the Jews of St. John's, Nfld.*, ISER, 1988.

While reading about them I was struck by our (by no means, unique) tendency to repeat the mistakes of the past. There's not enough time here to provide a comprehensive analysis of why the first colonies failed but we know that there were at least two outstanding reasons. One is the striking lack of *capital,* or assets that can be invested for profit; this was the case with Sir William Vaughan's colony at Trepassey and it is detailed in Dr. Nemec's article. The other reason for the plantations' failure was their over-emphasis on agriculture. In most cases, the soil resources were not rich enough to sustain successful agricultural development and if a colony were to succeed, involvement in the much more bountiful fishery was a prerequisite. In the late 19th century Newfoundlanders again made this error by neglecting to focus development efforts on marine resources, as Iceland did. This is not to say that agriculture cannot work in Newfoundland (far from it!) but that it could not be the cornerstone of economic development as it was in the plantations in 17th century New England: Newfoundland's resource endowment dictated this.

Let me note that while Guy's and Vaughan's colonies failed, the settlement of Newfoundland itself did not; beginning in the 1630s onwards a small year-round fishery began to develop on the Avalon Peninsula and then elsewhere on the island. Not surprisingly, given the experience in New England, the British government and the West Country merchants opposed settlement in Newfoundland; they were astute enough to realize that it would eventually lead to demands for economic and political independence. Their answer to this fear was to enact legislation to prohibit settlement, beginning in 1634. The Western Charter, as it was known, was introduced and then revised several times over the next decades to ensure that Newfoundland would be "settler-free." Its history is outlined below.

During most of the 1600s the British government was sympathetic toward the West Country merchants and their 'adventurers', or migratory fishermen. But that I am writing this and you are reading this attests to the fact that the Charter ultimately failed. When it became clear that laws passed two thousand miles away in London were not effective, armed conflict broke out between the increasingly desperate adventurers and the year-round settlers. Finally, the British government relented in 1677. This happened because it became clear it was in England's interest to finally allow permanent settlement in Newfoundland (England's motives and behaviour were typical of an imperialist power). This done, the Crown proceeded to ignore the people of Newfoundland for as long as it possibly could.

Table 1
History of the Western Charter
issued by Privy Council, England

Year	Provision
1634	Grants jurisdiction over English fishermen at Newfoundland to West Country mayors. Gives fishing admirals jurisdiction over crew members and coastal residents. Gives fishing admirals strategic property rights (based on a 'first come, first served' policy).
1637	Year-round residents are not allowed to live within six miles of the coastline. States that fishermen would be forever free from the jurisdiction of any Newfoundland Government that might emerge.
1661	Ships trading to Newfoundland are not permitted to carry persons who intend to settle there.
1670	20 new clauses, including: * No fishermen are allowed to stay in Newfoundland after fishing is ended * No ship may carry persons to Newfoundland who are not members of the ship's company
1676	Planters may not cut wood or reside within 6 miles of coastline.

Source: the author. Adapted from information contained in Matthews (1988) and Rowe, *History of Newfoundland* (1980).

What do you think were the reasons for the withdrawal of the Western Charter? A host of socio-economic factors were responsible. One was that the powers-that-be recognized that the settlers complemented the activities of the migratory fishermen. Keith Matthews quoted one record:[5]

> They protected equipment during the winter, relieved crews who arrived suffering from frostbite or scurvy, and prepared lumber, oars and boats which were sold to the fishing ships at extremely reasonable prices.

In addition to this, the British government was afraid that France would be able to stretch its North American acquisitions to include the island of Newfoundland. Permanent settlers would be one measure to counteract any French overtures.

Having been at a disadvantage for so long, the settlers did not outnumber the migratory fishermen until a century later! Reportedly, there were only 800 people in Newfoundland in 1710; 1800 in 1738; and 3400 in 1756. Certainly population growth was exceedingly slow, right up until the 1800s. You may have already thought of one of the primary reasons for this: the lack of women. There is not a lot of information available about female settlement in Newfoundland but we can be sure that women were rare in the early decades/centuries of settlement on the island. Migratory fishermen also returned to England and Ireland because of the their family ties there and the dearth of winter employment in Newfoundland.

Between 1760 and 1820, Newfoundland enjoyed something of a growth spurt due to factors internal and external to island society. First of all, new industries were established in the late 1700s; finally there were significant possibilities for year-round employment. Just as, or more, important, was the influx of Irish people beginning in approximately 1750. These people felt the pressures of overpopulation vis-à-vis land resources in Ireland and they flocked to Newfoundland. Keith Matthews found that in 1814 alone over 10,000 people came over from Ireland. By 1816, the population of Newfoundland had swelled

---

5 From Nemec, 1980, p. 37.

to about 50,000 people. This slow growth shows that the repeal of the Western Charter was not in itself enough to promote permanent settlement in Newfoundland. Still, I see the Western Charter as a flavourful part of our history. I feel certain that the ban on settlement has had a large effect on the Newfoundland culture and psyche. This segment of our history also had a long-term influence on the class system that has characterized Newfoundland society.

Sociological terms

Adventurers—migratory fishermen from the West Country and Southeast Ireland.

Capital—assets that can be invested for profit.

Livyer—a person who settled in Newfoundland to live year-round.

Plantation—an economic enterprise, usually agricultural in nature, set up by colonists. E.g., John Guy's "colony" at Cupids.

Lecture 3

Irish migration to Newfoundland

Prominent economist John Kenneth Galbraith has pointed out that there are two main forms of poverty: that which afflicts the few (case poverty); and that which afflicts the many (mass poverty). Case poverty is an aberration or exception in a society that is generally affluent; a family that depends on social assistance is an example of this. Mass poverty, on the other hand, is a complicated phenomenon that represents the total malfunctioning of the economic order and, therefore, society. Mass poverty is common in Third World countries, such as Guatemala, Uganda and Thailand, to name a few. We in the rich countries are accommodated or used to increasing income and material improvements in our lives. This contrasts with those in the Third World, most of whom are accommodated to what Galbraith calls the *equilibrium of poverty*, including the hopelessness of their economic situation.

In other words, most people will not try to improve their lives because there are few means of escape. Also, risk aversion, the unwillingness to take chances, is high; this is a rational adaptation to their circumstances, as risk-taking (such as investing in more advanced technology) can have dire consequences, such as hunger or death. This applies to people who live at what we call a *subsistence* level. There is, however, a *non-accommodating minority* in poor societies; in other words, there is always a small number of people who are willing to take risks in the hope of economic gains.

For these people, migration is often the optimal solution. When in the late 1700s and early 1800s, poverty became increasingly widespread in rural Ireland, migration was a solution that many people chose. Approximately one-third of Newfoundland's present population is descended from these people. For much of the rest of this lecture I will rely on MUN geographer John J. Mannion's work on Irish settlements in Eastern Canada (see bibliography), especially the Avalon Peninsula in Newfoundland.

Both Galbraith and Mannion agree that the main reason for Irish out-migration was economic distress at home. There were a few reasons for increasing poverty in Ireland during the period under study:

1. a dramatic population increase after 1770;
2. land re-organization schemes that led to tenant farmer evictions;
3. a lack of industry to absorb the displaced people; and
4. minor famines.

According to Mannion, agrarian riots became common after 1815, providing more incentive for people to leave Ireland.

Who were the Irish immigrants to Newfoundland?

Very often when we think of people immigrating to Canada or the U.S. we picture large European families or three generations of West Indian families. In the case of Ireland, emigration was a highly individualistic solution to economic distress. It was almost always the single individual or parent-child (nuclear) family that moved to Newfoundland. The extended family remained important in Ireland but it was in decline during this time. As Mannion points out:[6]

> Neither the dispersed farms that were mainly the product of landlord reorganization nor the indigenous joint holdings that all too often had been

[6] Mannion, p. 16.

> subdivided to minuscule proportions could support all the sons, but it rarely became necessary for the entire extended family to depart.

In fact, most of the emigrants were between 15 and 25 years old. They were single individuals or members of unrelated nuclear families. My own inkling is that more men than women immigrated to Newfoundland; it is probable that a few unmarried women under age 25 would have travelled to Newfoundland on their own with their husbands or to act as 'servants'.

They left behind a society that was comprised of three main classes:

1. the small farmers, the most numerous group;
2. landless labourers; and
3. rural craftspeople, such as blacksmiths and carpenters.

In general the landless labourers did not have enough resources to invest in travel across the Atlantic. The majority of those who came to Newfoundland were from the class of small farmers, the group that was most affected and even displaced by the reorganization of the land. The second largest proportion of immigrants were the artisans or craftspeople mentioned above.

The migration

It was not until the early 1800s that Irish settlements were established along Newfoundland's Cape Shore,[7] an area renowned for its Irish cultural flavour even today. In 1802, an Irish fisherman called John Skerry set up home in Ship Cove, ten miles south of Placentia. Mannion provides a colourful description of the early days:[8]

---

[7] The Cape Shore extends from Trepassey on the Southern Avalon Peninsula to Long Harbour at the head of Placentia Bay.

[8] Mannion, p. 18.

> From the beginning of the 18th century West Countrymen, (from Southwest England) who fished for cod each summer on the Grand Banks of Newfoundland, called at Waterford on their outbound journey to purchase provisions and enlist labourers for the season. Placentia was one of the major destinations for this seasonal Irish movement, yet no permanent Irish settlements were established on the Cape Shore until the beginning of the 19th century. By this time a Waterford merchant family, {the Sweetmans}, controlled the Placentia fishing trade and annually transported hundreds of Irishmen, some of whom stayed on during the winter to cut timber for boat building. Local folk tradition on the Cape Shore asserts that most of the Irishmen who first settled there fished for {the Sweetmans} and worked as winter men before settling down. In 1794 four men who were shipwrecked on Cape St. Mary's...wandered along the coat for four days without seeing a single settlement.

The majority of those who moved to the Cape Shore came from the southern Irish counties of Waterford, Wexford and Tipperary. Of all the groups of Irish immigrants in eastern Canada, the Cape Shore immigrants were the most isolated ethnically. With the exception of about thirty English inhabitants of Placentia, there were no non-Irish settlers along the entire Cape Shore in 1836. Mannion asserts that most of these people and their descendants probably lived their whole lives without contact with non-Irish Newfoundlanders. The case of the Irish in St. John's was different as the city had a large English population before the Irish migration. It's likely that daily contact was norm because these two groups were concentrated in a small geographical area. In fact, St. John's was the main destination for most Irish immigrants; their city population increased from 2,000 in 1794 to 14,000 forty years later. The scale of this influx led government to actively encourage agricultural settlements in rural parts of Newfoundland.

In his discussion of Irish and Scottish migration to North America, Galbraith concludes that migration solved the economic problems of both those who left and those who stayed behind, where the equilibrium of poverty was permanently weakened. Migration, he says, was an effective solution because it responded to the problems of accommodation and the equilibrium of poverty. The non-accommodating minority who left contributed invaluably to the economies of their new countries by filling demands for labour and/or creating jobs, for example. According to Galbraith, "All who moved, almost without exception, bettered their own position."[9]

Sociological Terms

Case poverty—poverty which afflicts the few, e.g., an individual or family. Usually seen in the affluent Western world.

Emigrate—to depart from one's homeland.

Equilibrium of poverty—while we in the West are accommodated (or used) to increasing affluence, the poor masses are accommodated to the equilibrium of poverty, the hopelessness of their economic situation.

Immigrate—to move into a new country.

Mass poverty—poverty that affects the majority of the population of an area, country, etc. Common in the Third World.

Non-accommodating minority—the few who reject the hopelessness of their economic situation. These are the people who emigrate.

Subsistence—means of support or livelihood. E.g., Irish farmers lived at a bare subsistence level.

---

9 Galbraith, p. 100.

Lecture 4

Class in Newfoundland society

The "merchant system" was entrenched in Newfoundland by the end of the 17th century. In those days Newfoundland planters had a merchant-client relationship with the merchants back in the English West Country. The merchant class (gradually, it became indigenous to the island and not centred in England) both supported and exploited the subordinate class of planters/settlers/fishermen. This system existed in some places up until Confederation with Canada in 1949 and even in rural Newfoundland today, there are vestiges of it left.

A lot has been said about the Water Street merchants and the outport merchants and they remain a controversial subject to many Newfoundlanders. Before we consider the question of whether or not the merchants constitute a class, let's define the term 'merchant' in the Newfoundland context. To do this we can look to an essay by historian Keith Matthews (Lecture XXIX, 1988). Matthews saw a "fish merchant proper" as:[10]

> ...a man who owned his own seagoing vessels and possessed the capacity to import goods into his own stores in Newfoundland, and to export fish directly

---

[10] Matthews, p. 177

> to the market abroad. This type were the prototype of the Water Street merchants of the 19th and early 20th century and although...they differed as individuals, they seemed to have generally possessed a certain common outlook on life.

The merchant was not an unmoving or unchanging figure throughout the centuries of European settlement in Newfoundland. As socio-economic circumstances and conditions changed in Newfoundland, so did the roles and functions of the merchants. For example, early in our history, the small-scale merchants were called *dealers* and many of them were planters or fishermen, just as their customers were. In these cases, then, there was some overlap between what we often perceive as two distinct classes. In addition to changes over time, at any given time there were all sorts of merchants in Newfoundland, as opposed to one type. It is inaccurate, then, to see merchants as a homogenous group.

In spite of this, there is a traditional merchant culture in Newfoundland. It makes sense that merchants shared a common world-view and belief system because their experiences of life were similar. Let's take a brief look at their yearly round of activities. Just as it was for the fishing families, the fishery was precarious and unpredictable for the merchants as well. In early January money was needed to buy goods from other countries and to repair ships for the upcoming season. Several months later the merchant (in the West Country or Newfoundland) would have to advance supplies on credit to the fishermen, not knowing whether the season would be successful. Because of the nature of fishing, many things could go wrong: weather, lack of fish, poor markets, and other factors that many of you are no doubt aware of. These difficulties were exacerbated by war which broke out occasionally in the 1700s and 1800s and which was largely fought at sea. Reportedly, in 1784 there were forty-four firms controlling the fishery; by 1810, only thirteen of them survived.[11] This shows how unstable and dangerous life in the fishing industry could be.

While we have tended to see the merchant as the villain of our

---

[11] Matthews, 1988, p. 179.

history, there is no doubt that the merchant's role was a pivotal one. In the words of Keith Matthews:[12]

> ...good or bad, settlement and fishing in Newfoundland depended absolutely upon the existence of merchants who alone possessed the money and shipping to import supplies and to export fish. Without them, the fishery must die, and the inhabitants starve.

In my view, there could have been more balanced structures playing the role that the merchants did in Newfoundland. But, as Matthews says, they had a monopoly over importing and exporting and so they occupied a crucial position in the system. Because the fishermen, as individuals, needed the merchants more than the merchants needed them, in my view the relationship was an unbalanced one in terms of economic and social power. Undoubtedly there were some kind and benevolent merchants (they liked to see themselves this way) but the system itself was weighted in the merchants' favour. Marxist analysts, for example, would see the system as an exploitive one.

We know through the work of historians and other social scientists that the merchants tended to be socially and politically conservative. Matthews says that they were "genuine free traders, competitive (and) independent" and that they resented government legislation in the fisheries. Because of the nature of the fishery, *speculators* were disliked; their risk-taking could easily upset the delicate balance in the industry. The thrift and conservative decision-making of the merchants no doubt was misunderstood by many Newfoundlanders who witnessed the merchants' relative affluence and saw their prudence as unnecessary. Certainly there was a gap between the merchants' perception of themselves and the way the fishing people viewed them. Yet in spite of the undercurrent of hostility, overt confrontations between the various classes were rare. For the most part, Newfoundlanders were deferential in their interactions with the merchants (and others in positions of power); perhaps this attitude developed because of the fishermen's constant

[12] Matthews, p. 177.

economic vulnerability, which was even greater than the merchants' and also subject to the merchants' will. Religion and gender are other areas that have divided Newfoundlanders into opposing groups—we'll discuss gender in particular in later lectures. Let's turn to urban Newfoundland now and the place of St. John's in our history.

Sociological Terms

Dealer—small-scale merchants operating early in Newfoundland history.

Merchant—in the Newfoundland context, the merchant had significant political and economic power. See Matthews' definition on pp. 21-22 of this book.

Speculator—a merchant who took economic risks in his business. A speculator was the exception among the merchant class and was disliked by other merchants.

Lecture 5

St. John's—Newfoundland's capital city in history

St. John's first appeared in written accounts in 1505 when it was a seasonal fishing station with an extremely well-protected harbour. Since then the harbour has always been central to the development of St. John's. Settlement developed around it and even in this, the jet age, dock and cargo work is a major source of employment in the city. The province's capital is home to over a quarter of our population and many thousands of people live in adjacent communities, such as Mount Pearl and Paradise. With the implementation of the municipal amalgamation program of the Wells government, St. John's now includes Goulds, Wedgewood Park and other places in its jurisdiction. Mount Pearl is literally surrounded by the capital and it is perhaps only a matter of time before it is swallowed up by the emerging 'super-city', as it has been called by both proponents and opponents of the amalgamation proposals.

One does not need to spend much time in Newfoundland before one becomes aware of St. John's status as the commercial, administrative and political centre of the province. The city stands above other Newfoundland towns and cities in terms of business activity and economic power. Additionally, it is the seat of the provincial government and the location of the main campus of our sole university, Memorial University of Newfoundland.

None of this is said to raise the ire of those of you from the rest of the province. In fact, one of the myths that I'd like to challenge here is that there is a great cultural divide between 'townies' and 'baymen' and that the two are separate entities. In my view, Newfoundlanders from all backgrounds make up a continuum of cultural experiences and there are more overlaps than there are gaps. This is a subject I would like to return to after we immerse ourselves in the history and development of St. John's as our capital city.

The slow ascendency of St. John's

Urban sociologists agree that communities generally develop slowly, over long periods of time through continuous changes affecting the people who live or trade in the nearby areas. It was not until the 1800s, then (long after its first written mention in 1505), that St. John's began to become entrenched as Newfoundland's capital. It was during this period that the city became the monopolizer of the fishery and seal hunt of the most populated East Coast and Labrador.

But as historian Keith Matthews labouriously pointed out in his work, there was nothing "God-given" about the prominence of St. John's. Even early on, St. John's itself had little economic importance; the town could not support a large population of people dependent on the inshore fishery. The strength of St. John's was in communications; the Old English Shore ran from Trepassey to Greenspond with St. John's right in the middle. It is this central position that secured the status of St. John's as Newfoundland's capital city.

For the remainder of this lecture I will rely primarily on material provided by Dr. Matthews from his very readable book, *Lectures on the History of Newfoundland, 1500–1830* (Breakwater, 1988). According to Matthews, the 'real beginning' of the city was in 1697 when, following King William's War, the Crown set up a military garrison at St. John's. It expanded greatly in the next twenty years and it prospered as the unofficial centre of communications and administration for the English shore. By 1720, most of the planters in St. John's had given up fishing and had opened taverns. The new pattern was that St. John's would become the centre of commerce while the fishery would grow up in areas outside the town. Today there are about 100 inshore fishermen in St. John's but, for the most part, the pattern persists.

According to Matthews, by 1775 St. John's was "clearly

dominant in all but purely economic functions".[13] Yet it did not *control* the outports, with the exception of nearby communities like Torbay and Petty Harbour. Most fishermen were supplied by merchants in their own areas. Indeed, in the last quarter of the 18th century, the richest merchants traded in Trinity, Harbour Grace, Carbonear, Ferryland, Placentia and Little Bay. These merchants had little or no contact with their counterparts in St. John's; they ordered their supplies from outside Newfoundland and marketed their fish directly.

The economic importance of St. John's was not established until the end of the Napoleonic Wars (1815). The American Revolution in 1777, too, had brought a number of changes that contributed to the rise of St. John's. These included:

1. the development of trade with Canada and the West Indies;
2. increasing numbers of tradespeople and dealers in St. John's;
3. the decay of the outports' economy which had been very intertwined with the West of England migratory fishery;
4. the growth of the Scottish trade to Newfoundland;
5. the transfer of English businesses to St. John's;
6. the growth of the Labrador fishery; and
7. the escalation of the sealing industry.

All these developments helped St. John's establish itself as the strongest financial and trading centre in Newfoundland.

From the presence of economic infrastructure and a burgeoning population sprang social, cultural and educational institutions. Perhaps not surprisingly, then, it was in St. John's that demands for political and social reform originated. Eventually, the city became the political capital on the island. The relatively educated and wealthy middle classes continued to migrate in from the outports as the rural-based merchant economy declined. As Matthews points out, it is quite ironic that St. John's reached its peak just as Corner Brook and other such centres were beginning to emerge. He says, "St. John's reached its height just as the development of the West

---

[13] Matthews, p. 168.

Coast and of non-fishing industries, combined with our entry into Canada and the decline of the fishery made it less natural as our capital."[14] In the next section, we will look more closely at society in St. John's, particularly in the modern day.

Table 2: The Rise of St. John's	
1505	First written account of St. John's, then a seasonal fishing station.
1697	English Crown builds fort, establishes military garrison at St. John's.
1713	St. John's clearly administrative and communications centre for English Shore.
1720	By now, few fishermen; more residents are owners/keepers.
1729	Crown creates naval governor and justice of the peace, all stationed in St. John's.
1730-1765	Establishment of criminal court, customs and naval officials in St. John's.
1777	American Revolution (see text).
1815	Napoleonic Wars end. By now, St. John's dominates Newfoundland in economic life.
1832	St. John's becomes the official political centre of the island.
1888	Municipal government set up in St. John's.
Source: the author. Adapted from information contained in Matthews (1988) and Rowe, *History of Newfoundland* (1980).	

[14] Matthews, p. 169.

Lecture 6

Society and social life in St. John's

Commercial St. John's

Commercial or mercantile capitalism is at the basis of the Newfoundland and North American economies. Capitalism is the process of buying and selling goods for profit. The distinguishing feature and core of the system is private property. To summarize then, capitalism is the process of buying goods at one price for the express purpose of selling them at a higher price in order to realize a profit. To become established as a capitalist, one has to put forward a significant initial outlay. Many sociologists would argue that the system is inherently unfair because only a small proportion of the population can afford an initial outlay. Those people who become capitalists are, therefore, in a minority. The majority of the population work for, or sell its labour to, the capitalists (or business people). This process occurs in St. John's, where most people would be considered members of the working or middle classes.

The mercantile system in St. John's is organized along the same lines as that of rural Newfoundland, only on a larger (and some would say, more impersonal) scale. While some outport merchants have been more successful than their urban counterparts (especially in monopoly situations), the economic opportunities in St. John's have been better, partly because of the relatively large population. In earlier lectures on Newfoundland society and culture (1980) sociologist Doug House outlined three features of mercantile life in St. John's. These are:

1. its close association with particular families;
2. the high rate of turnover among larger firms; and
3. the close interconnection between capitalist success and leadership in other social (e.g., political) spheres.

Traditionally, local family firms have been prominent in commercial St. John's; some examples are Bowrings, the Harvey group of companies, and the various enterprises of the Ayre family. The patriarchs of these families were thought of as the city's leaders in all municipal affairs.

Two trends are evident in more recent years, one beginning earlier than the other. First of all, there has been some turnover in the leading capitalist families in this century. The "nouveau riche" element (the successful upwardly mobile capitalists) includes, for example, Chester Dawe and Craig Dobbin. Another trend, disturbing to many, is the growing presence of national and multi-national retail chains like Woolco and McDonald's. Consumers at the Avalon Mall in St. John's shop at many of the same stores as the consumers in the Eaton Centre in Toronto or the West Edmonton Mall. (The decline of local ownership and commercial downtown St. John's is one consequence of this.) Let's now look at the people who make up the community of St. John's.

Population and settlement

I've often heard it said that if you take the baymen out of St. John's there would be nobody left. As with much of conventional wisdom this is an exaggeration, but there is some truth in it. Like many pre- and semi-industrial towns, St. John's did not reproduce itself throughout much of its history. In other words, each generation of "townies" did not produce a sufficient number of surviving "townies" to keep the population level or to increase it. Yet we know that the number of people living in St. John's has increased steadily for decades. For example, it was less than 30,000 in 1901 but had grown to approximately 50,000 by the time of Confederation with Canada. How is this so? The answer is through the constant influx or immigration of rural people. This is the way that most pre- and semi-industrial towns in Europe and elsewhere reproduced themselves. Traditionally, in St. John's there has been a higher proportion of people of working age. This is evidence that rural workers move into the city.

In St. John's, then, many people have one or both parents from 'around the bay,' meaning rural Newfoundland. (This is true in my own case. My family comes from Little Bay on the Burin Peninsula, although I was raised in St. John's.) Even for those who are second or third generation townies, there are often rural roots at some point in their family history. These rural people moved in from all over Newfoundland for economic and other reasons. For example, I know a couple who left a Placentia Bay community because there didn't seem to be a promising future in the fishing industry. Some of my cousins came into the city for educational reasons (e.g., to attend the Cabot Institute) and decided to settle here after graduation. Some rural people wanted to change their social status and moved to the city with its relatively wide range of occupational opportunities.

In some areas of the capital city and environs (the surrounding areas), there are clusters of people from a particular bay or part of the province. For example, it's well known that large numbers of people from Bonavista Bay settled in the Mount Pearl area. One area of St. John's that I lived in is often called "Little Bonavista". This is a social pattern that is mirrored in other urban centres—hundreds of former Bell Islanders live in Cambridge, Ontario, for example; while thousands of Pakistanis are clustered in the East End of London, England. It is probable that this pattern is declining in St. John's but there is no doubt that it was a common phenomenon throughout the city's history. It was certainly a practice during the resettlement era in Newfoundland.

Keeping all this in mind, it becomes clear that the townie-baymen conflict is shrouded in myth. It is a falsehood that the people of St. John's live in a separate world from the rest of the province, or that they constitute their own society. It is also erroneous to view Newfoundland as made up of "St. John's and rural Newfoundland (or the rest of the province)." While there are differences between urban and rural communities, we should view the communities in our province as on a rural-urban continuum. That is, urbanites live in Corner Brook, Gander and elsewhere, while the non-urban citizens of Newfoundland live in a wide range of communities. These include outports accessible only by boat (such as Grey River); semi-industrialized towns like Baie Verte and Marystown; fishing communities near urban areas (Petty Harbour, for example); and many other kinds of settlements. These places have much in common (starting with their status as *not* the capital city!) but it is important to remember that there are also a great deal of differences between them.

To view the social composition of Newfoundland communities another way, we can say that there is much continuity between urban and rural life in Newfoundland, perhaps more so than in other North American states and provinces. We have only to remember the transplanted outport people to see this. Many urbanites take part in 'rural' activities such as moose-hunting, while many rural people regularly use the commercial, medical and other services in St. John's. In addition, there are significant differences between groups of people in St. John's itself. It is a mistake to lump all townies into one category when we consider class, religion and other social characteristics. It is just not true, for example, that everyone in St. John's is rich—the workers at the city's food banks will attest to this. This is not an inference that should be drawn simply because most of the province's wealthiest people live in St. John's.

To close off this lecture, I'd like to introduce you to a community within a community—Georgetown, St. John's. I hope this gives you a picture of life in one of the city's older, more close-knit neighbourhoods. (The following is an excerpt from a paper of mine.)

Georgetown: one of the human faces of St. John's

Georgetown has existed as a distinctive neighbourhood for over 100 years. In its early days it was on the outskirts of St. John's but now it is very much a part of the inner city. (As one woman of sixty remarked: "When I was a little girl here we were way out in the country.") I grew up mainly in Georgetown and this lecture on my childhood community dawns from ethnographic research I did there a decade ago.

The land was first owned by George Winter (hence, the name) who rented it out. By 1858, the name Georgetown had come into common use. The streets of the neighbourhood were narrow as they were originally designed for horse and buggy. (Many are now one-way thoroughfares.) Most of the houses are attached on one or both sides and tend to be two or three storeys high (although there is the odd bungalow). Not surprisingly very few homes have front lawns, unlike suburban St. John's, and many lack driveways. In most of the fifteen blocks in Georgetown, there are narrow winding dirt lanes, a legacy of the days when livestock roamed the area. In a 1977 survey carried out for the Neighbourhood Improvement Committee, it was found that there were 2198 people living in Georgetown. I would think that the population remains roughly the same as there have been few major alterations to dwelling houses. It's possible that the population may have decreased somewhat because of declining birth rates in Newfoundland.

Social solidarity in Georgetown

Unlike as in many rural communities the occupations held by Georgetown residents are diversified; the community is, after all, part of the capital city of St. John's. Living in the neighbourhood are professors, secretaries, servers, pensioners, construction workers, salespeople, students, unemployed, social service recipients and people in many other fields. The majority of these people are non-professional workers, however. Historically, Georgetown has a higher unemployment rate and a lower mean income than other parts of the city. When I was growing up there, most people had low to moderate incomes and were members of the working class. There were some well-off people, such as doctors, who lived on the border streets of Georgetown. The community has become increasingly gentrified in recent years and class divisions have been exacerbated. Many Georgetown residents have a cynical attitude toward the incoming professionals or "yuppies." They see these people as living in the area for reasons of fashion or trendiness. Reportedly,

Georgetown has the highest rate of home ownership in St. John's, despite its other somewhat depressing socio-economic indicators.

I have mentioned class divisions in Georgetown and you may have noted that there is not the kind of economic interdependence that exists in rural communities. For these reasons community solidarity may not be as strong in Georgetown as it is in some outports. However, it does exist and I'd suggest it is very strong by urban standards. One reason for this is that Georgetown is geographically small and therefore people can get to know each other easily. Another is that there are a significant number of extended families, in one or more households, living in the area. When I was a teenager, I knew two sisters who lived across the street from each other. Another woman lived "a hop, skip and a jump" away from her two daughters and nine of her grandchildren from two separate households. In these cases, people interact with their relatives and their relatives' neighbours. As a result a sense of community emerges.

While there is a transient population in Georgetown (e.g., students) it seems that a majority of people have lived there for a long time. I know several people who have lived in Georgetown all their lives and would wince at the thought of moving. In the late 1970s, the Neighbourhood Improvement Committee found that 75% of the residents wanted to stay there. Georgetown is "near everything;" such as downtown, a supermarket, schools and bus routes. The fact that the community is largely homogenous enhances solidarity, too. About three-quarters of Georgetown people are Roman Catholic and the nearby Basilica, its priests and organizations are at the apex of the community. There are also six Roman Catholic schools in the neighbourhood or bordering it. For all these reasons, social solidarity is a feature of Georgetown life. Although, surrounded by the rest of St. John's, it cannot be all-encompassing.

Forms of social interaction

What I call "store interaction" is an important part of social life for many people. The storekeepers are well-known and friendly (one even asked my friend, new to the neighbourhood, if he would be interested in going out with her friend!) The stores often serve as gossip centres; you often hear someone say "I heard it down to B's." Gossip can spread very fast in Georgetown! In this respect, the community is similar to a smaller Newfoundland outport.

Although the men gather in the stores almost as much as the women, they had their own exclusive meeting place, the Georgetown Pub, until eleven years ago. This pub did not allow women inside. In fact, it was, allegedly, the last pub in North America to operate solely for one sex (excluding homosexual clubs). This points to the patriarchal nature of the community. The schools were segregated by sex, too, when I was a student in the 1970s. Today the Georgetown Pub is open to members of both sexes but it hasn't quite managed to shake its reputation as "a hard place."

The streets themselves become a gathering place during warm summer evenings. As in most North American communities, teenagers like "hanging out" on street corners or outside stores flirting and smoking. As young girls, we would go for endless walks around the block. Older people also use the streets as a meeting place during the summer. Unlike as in the case of teenagers, there is some sex segregation with men talking to men and women socializing with women. There are a few small parks in Georgetown but there is no indoor play or community centre. We used to skate at Memorial Stadium, a twenty minute walk away (more if there was 'skylarking').

Most of the teenagers I knew went to Holy Heart School (for girls) or Brother Rice (for boys; both of these are now integrated by sex). Many of us were involved with school organizations like Allied Youth or the Young Christian Leadership Organization. Other young people's social lives centred around the Church. They were members of the Basilica Youth Council or the Basilica Youth Choir.

Social problems

At this point you may be reminded of "Leave it to Beaver" or some other 1950s sitcom, but very few homes were like these sitcoms, in Georgetown or elsewhere. Sometimes the difficulties facing Georgetown seemed overwhelming: vandalism, unemployment, poor housing, frequent teenage pregnancy and rampant alcoholism and family violence. In my childhood years, there was also a significant problem with illegal drugs; the lanes provided a perfect place to deal in drugs. For this reason, plain clothes police officers infiltrated Georgetown each summer, in cars and on foot. This contributed to the feelings of persecution and insecurity many of the youth felt. A few of them even saw the class implications of law enforcement; I remember one boy saying "why don't they hang around Bally Haly (a rich St. John's suburb)?" Throughout this course we'll talk a lot more about communities in Newfoundland. At this point you should begin to think about the sociology of your own community.

References for Unit 1

- David Alexander. *The Decay of Trade: An Economic History of the Newfoundland Saltfish Trade, 1935–1965,* ISER, MUN, St. John's, 1979.
- David Alexander. "The Economic History of a Province," *The Canadian Forum,* Vol. 53, No. 638 (March, 1974), pp. 26–27.
- Peter Evans. *Dependent Development: The Alliance of Multinational, State and Local Capital in Brazil,* Princeton University Press, Princeton, NJ, 1979.
- Bryant Fairley, Colin Leys, James Sacouman, eds. *Restructuring and Resistance: Perspectives from Atlantic Canada,* Garamond Press, Toronto, 1990.
- Andre Gunder Frank. *Capitalism and Underdevelopment in Latin America: Historical Studies of Chile and Brazil,* Monthly Review Press, New York, 1969.
- John Kenneth Galbraith. *The Nature of Mass Poverty,* Penguin, 1979.
- Maura Hanrahan. "Georgetown, St. John's: A Community Study", MUN, St. John's, March, 1982.
- Bjorn Hettne. *Development Theory and the Three Worlds,* Longman Scientific and Technical, Harlow, UK, 1990.
- John J. Mannion. *Irish Settlements in Eastern Canada: A Study of Cultural Transfer and Adaptation,* University of Toronto Press, 1974.
- Keith Matthews. *Lectures on the History of Newfoundland, 1500–1830,* Breakwater, St. John's, 1988. (Copyright ©1988 Mary Kathleen Matthews).

- Frederick Rowe. *A History of Newfoundland & Labrador,* McGraw-Hill Ryerson, Toronto, 1980.
- Mark Shrimpton and Christopher A. Sharpe. "An Inner City in Decline: St. John's, Newfoundland" in *Soc./Anthro./Folklore 2230 Book of Readings,* Newfoundland Society and Culture, by J.D. House (ed.), MUN, St. John's, 3rd edition, 1984.

Unit Two

Grassroots politics in Newfoundland

Introduction

When the word 'politics' is mentioned, many of us visualize government, whether it is on a municipal, provincial or national level. In our discussion of politics for "Newfoundland Society and Culture" we will use a much broader concept of politics. Thus, when I refer to 'politics' in the following lectures I am thinking of a wide range of power relationships within Newfoundland society. These relations of power are structural characteristics of all Newfoundland institutions (and institutions in other societies), such as schools, the law and its enforcement agencies and the state. Power is a feature of all relationships in society, including class, gender and race relationships; therefore, 'politics' is a constant feature of our everyday lives in society.

It is fair to say that the majority of sociologists believe that those who hold power, in its multiplicity of forms, desire to keep it; for this reason, they have a vested interest in preserving the status quo (the existing situation). (At this point an interesting exercise would be to consider what political relationships you are involved in and to reflect upon your position in them.) Not only do those in power wish to retain their authority and privilege, but very often they will deliberately work to prevent even the most incremental of changes, not to mention more structural alterations. Many sociologists see resistance to change as an unwillingness to redistribute resources. Allegedly, the pursuit of power is not a natural characteristic of human beings or human nature; instead, it is a social construction, constructed out of the organization and distribution of resources and the social schema of power and privilege. If we are to accept that power is *not* a fundamental part of the human psyche, then it follows that altering power relationships in society is not impossible. This is the hope of those who are involved in social movements.

Institutions will function according to the ideologies and ideas of those who wield power within those institutions. They will resist change whether it is pushed for by an individual or demanded by an organized group, such as a union. Let's look at unions for a moment. Unions collectivize the process of negotiation and give workers a way to gain a measure of power in a relationship that is decidedly unequal—the relationship between workers and owners/managers who control/own the workplace.[1] Employers resist change by promoting anti-strike legislation, for example, or using replacement workers (called "scabs" by union members). Unions themselves are an example of *social movements,* which we may define as "collective attempts to change some or all aspects of society." At this point it would be interesting to consider which, if any, groups in your community constitute social movements. Social movements are political (though not necessarily partisan, associated with a political party such as the Liberals) because they are concerned with questions of power and the power structures in society.[2] If you were to ask me for examples of social movements in Newfoundland, I would point to the women's suffrage movement, the groups currently protesting tentative plans to build a garbage incinerator in Long Harbour, and the Fishermen's Union, among others. While many social movements are led by famous intellectuals or activists, others spring up from the "grassroots" of society. Let's focus on these now.

---

1 Newfoundland is one of the most unionized provinces in Canada.

2 Later in this section we will elaborate on our discussion of social movements. We will also look at a couple of social movements in Newfoundland in detail.

In this particular discussion of politics in Newfoundland, I have chosen to focus on *grassroots* political movements; that is, movements and protests that originate among or are carried on by the 'common' or working class people. In such movements, leadership is *not* provided by a social or economic elite and those heading the movement very often are more organizers than leaders (this is true in the case of the Burin protest line as we shall see, and it is more characteristic of women's groups than of men's). In this unit, then, we will look at organizations with *political aims* such as the Fishermen's Protective Union which sought to bring about major changes to the economic system in which fishermen operated. *Political parties*, such as the Liberal Reform party or the Progressive Conservatives, are not our focus here.

I have decided to emphasize grassroots politics for a number of reasons, some pragmatic and others relating to my own interests. These reasons (in no particular order) are:

1. There is a wealth of information elsewhere on what we think of as conventional politics;
2. Historically, academics have tended to neglect the political activities of the working class and other marginal groups;
3. I hope to help students develop an awareness of just how broad the concepts of power and politics are; and
4. I have a particular academic interest in social movements.

With this in mind, we will look at the struggles of women in Newfoundland politics, to begin with.

Lecture 1

Women and politics—a separate sphere?

I have decided to include a lecture specifically on Women and Politics in Newfoundland because, despite our being half the population, there is so little known about this topic. And not just that—it's so interesting. Did you know that women here were fighting for the right to vote as far back as 1850? Newfoundland women have a colourful "herstory," even in areas like politics which we so often associate with men.

When we think of politics in Newfoundland, most people picture the House of Assembly, our provincial legislature, or a Liberal or PC party convention. As I write this (in 1992), there are only two female MHAs, Lynn Verge (PC) and Patt Cowan (Lib.) out of a possible fifty-two. Since 1928 only seven women have sat in the Newfoundland House of Assembly in St. John's. The woman who first broke into this province's patriarchal politics was Lady Helena Squires, wife of then Prime Minister, Sir Richard Squires. From Little Bay Islands, Lady Helena was elected to represent Lewisporte for the Liberals in 1928. She won easily, garnering 81% of the vote. Lady Helena is remembered for her forthrightness and her hard work; one of her charitable activities was providing help to unwed mothers.

Lady Helena was elected a few short years after women finally won the right to vote in Newfoundland in 1925.[3] Women did not

---

3 The vote was granted to women over 25 (men could vote at 21) because young women were seen as "flighty".

achieve their goal easily and it was not until fifty years after Lady Helena's election that another woman followed her into the House of Assembly. The struggle by women for suffrage was difficult and it was long. The first demonstration or march that I have heard about took place in St. John's in 1881 and involved fifty women. The women who marched were seen as militant and unfeminine and they were, not surprisingly, attacked in the local press. Many people felt that women were out to emasculate men, to steal power from them and oppress them. These views were held in other countries where there were active women suffrage movements, including Britain and the United States. The Newfoundland Prime Minister, Edward Morris, articulated the opinion of perhaps a majority of the population when he said, "If they once took woman from the proper sphere, they might not be able to put her back again." Morris was perceptive in realizing that participation in politics would enhance women's roles in other aspects of life.

According to Prime Minister Morris, the proper sphere for women was the home. Feminist scholars tell us that women operate in the private sphere while men operate in the public sphere (political life, business, etc.). Certainly in Morris' day, women's participation in decision-making in the public realm was severely restricted. (The lecture on the sexual division of labour elaborates on this.) My own belief is that the individual should be free to choose to participate in whichever realm he or she wants to, regardless of gender. This would have been considered a radical view in nineteenth century Newfoundland. In some quarters in twentieth century Newfoundland it may still be seen as radical. A recent article in the Newfoundland women's magazine, *Waterlily*, laments the stark lack of information on women and politics in this province. I'll quote from that article:[4]

> For all that is written, it might be assumed that women did nothing. But that we know to be not true...Women have for hundreds of years been fighting for one cause or another. The challenge is

[4] "So little information about women in politics", *Waterlily*, Vol. 2, Number 4, St. John's, 1991, p. 11.

> to move that energy into the political arena. It's a challenge we must move quickly on.

As the authors of that article point out, our foremothers have been very involved in political lobbying. They've also been active, the backbone even, of church and community groups in Newfoundland. So while women's political activities have not been confined to local or community politics, it is here that they have been the most influential. We've talked about Lady Helena Squires who was outstanding in our herstory. But most women haven't had the socio-economic advantages (class, wealth, power) that she enjoyed. Most of our foremothers who have been involved in politics (at whatever level) have not been from the upper classes—think about your own service groups or municipal government. In fact, their achievements are all the more remarkable given the family and work responsibilities so many of them had. For the rest of the lecture, we'll take a closer look at female political culture in Newfoundland.

We saw the negative reaction that Newfoundland suffragettes met with and a couple of decades later the situation had not changed significantly. Early in this century a petition with 1700 signatures demanding women's suffrage was presented to parliament. It is important to note the role that class played; many of the activists strove only for votes for women property owners. (When "universal suffrage" was introduced here and elsewhere, it was usually property owners, and not all men, who became enfranchised.) One of the female campaigners put her memories on paper:[5]

> For years we agitated gently. I accompanied Mrs. McNeil, as her lieutenant, when she interviewed Prominent People. One well-known old gentleman told Mrs. Mitchell: 'Go home, madame, and learn to bake bread.' 'I bake excellent bread' was her reply. Surprising to find some otherwise delightful people

---

5 "Current Events Club—Women Suffrage—Newfoundland Society of Art". The Book of Newfoundland, ed. Joseph R. Smallwood, Vol. 1, pp. 194-201.

fly into terrific rages and order us out of their offices, when they learnt what our mission was.

The suffragettes reported that the politicians of the day feared that women would overrun parliament and take their positions. There was so much of this sort of fear that some civil servants married to suffragettes were told they would lose their jobs if their wives continued the campaign. Eventually the suffragettes were successful and shortly afterwards Lady Helena became the MP for Lewisporte. Before women won the parliamentary vote, they had obtained the municipal vote (for property owners only). According to one suffragette, every woman who could tried to buy a garage or a shed. In doing the research for this lecture I came across references to "the Women's Party." This group ran two candidates (that I know of) in the 1925 municipal election: Fanny McNeil and Mae Kennedy. Julia Salter Earle, the well-known social reformer, ran on the Labour ticket but all three women lost. (Julia's campaign slogan has earned a place in Newfoundland folklore: "Vote for Julia—She Won't Fool Ya!")

At this point I'd like to turn to modern female political culture. For this part of the lecture I'll rely on an article by MUN sociologist Marilyn Porter. It's called " 'A Tangly Bunch': The Political Culture of Outport Women in Newfoundland."[6] Porter studied the political lives of women on the Southern Shore of the Avalon Peninsula in the early 1980s. She found that most women were actively involved in at least one association while the majority had a number of such involvements. The main organizations were the Ladies Auxiliary (Church), the Legion, the Women's Institute, the Kinettes and Darts League. Porter tells us that these groups created a social space to which all women were attracted. She also says that to associate *as women* was seen in a positive light; in fact, all-female social events seemed to be more popular than mixed-sex ones.

One of Porter's more interesting observations has to do with the complex set of connections between all the communities of the

---

[6] This article can be found in the companion book to this one, *Through a Mirror Dimly: Essays on Newfoundland Society and Culture.*

100 mile long shore. All the outports were small enough, within themselves, to allow face to face contact between all the members, but at the same time they were part of a geographically spread-out community, i.e., the entire Southern Shore. The social system extended to provincial and federal structures so that places like Aquaforte were ultimately connected to Ottawa. According to Porter it was the women who maintained and cemented these connections. This is because "women start with an inherently 'wider world' than the men"[7] in that upon marriage they move away their family and community of origin, unlike men. And, because of their high frequency of involvements with various organizations, the Southern Shore women had many opportunities to meet women from neighbouring outports. These meetings took place regularly and on a structured basis.

This contrasts sharply with the past when women were isolated because transport by sea was considered to be part of men's domain. Porter points out that:

> ...the coming of all-weather roads and nearly universal car ownership have transformed *women's* mobility. The men still dominate the terra jet and skidoo trips to the woods; but the women have taken to the roads."[8]

This meant that women's public activity extended beyond their immediate community. Porter thinks (although I disagree) that this gave the women a virtual monopoly over the informal communication network. Yet, in spite of this and their high level of public activity (compared to men's), this sociologist concludes that it is the male groups that dominated those public expressions of what is commonly called politics. Your job as students of Newfoundland society and culture is to decide if the findings of this study might apply to Newfoundland as a whole. And then you should ask, if Porter's observations about female politics are correct, why is the situation as it is?

---

7 Porter, 1982, p. 11.

8 *Ibid.*

One of the most valid points made in this study of Southern Shore women is that these women have made a significant contribution to Newfoundland politics (although not necessarily in the sense of politics as we usually mean it is, i.e., party politics). And women have developed useful political skills like networking. In addition to this, and as we'll see in later lectures, women have traditionally been a crucial part of the Newfoundland economy. Women have always been responsible for fish processing as well as shop, post office, and home and family management. But in the case of Newfoundland society, economic activity does not equal political power. We've had few women representatives in elected government offices and that economic contribution by women has not been sufficiently recognized.

With this in mind it is perhaps not surprising that the women of the Southern Shore felt that 'politics,' as it's conventionally seen, was uninteresting and depressing and that nothing could be done about it. Pollsters regularly report that as citizens we feel fed up with and cynical about our politicians. This may be more true for women who remain largely outside traditional politics.

Earlier, I said if the women of the Southern Shore are any indication, then women have considerable skills and significant potential power. Yet they don't always use this power to oppose the actions of the state or business. (Think about whether or not this is true of the women in your area.) The women of the Southern Shore "have turned their backs on politics as they understand it"[9] and have constructed their own separate political culture. Their achievements should be discovered, celebrated, as part of our history and herstory, and built upon in the future.

The article which follows details a recent political struggle in Newfoundland and Canada: the 1990 fight to have funding to women's centres across the country reinstated. The movement was successful in accomplishing its stated goal but also in winning popular support for feminist causes and educating the public about issues affecting women. It will give you a 'more concrete' understanding of women in the political process.

---

9 *Ibid.*, p. 22.

Introduction to 'This is democracy?: Reflections on the occupation experience'

Many of you will remember that in 1990, the federal government eliminated its $1.2 million operating grant to Women's Centres across Canada. The response was a spontaneous protest on the part of women's groups in every province, but especially in Newfoundland. Eventually most of the funding was reinstated after a high-profile, concentrated protest. Before you read the article included here, detailing the story of the protest, the following introduction will help put it in context.

The majority of sociologists agree that the modern women's movement (of the past 20–25 years) has had a significant impact on modern society. They would point to: changes in the traditional sexual division of labour in the home; to women's expanded roles in the workplace; to changes in the perceptions of sexual crime; and other sociological developments. At the base of all these changes were some revolutionary (for their time) ideas. According to the authors of *Feminist Organizing for Change* (1988) two of these ideas in particular have been central to the women's movement. (This applies to the movement in all of North America and Western Europe, including Newfoundland.) These ideas are: the 'personal is political'; and 'sisterhood is powerful'! Together, they form the basis of feminist ideology and the women's movement. To understand what the movement seeks, then, we will look at each of these ideas in turn.

At its basic level, the notion that the 'personal is political' means that gender relations are proscribed rather than the result of individual choices or laws of nature. For example, feminists would claim that women would not choose to be entirely responsible for housework, given the choice, and nor are they designed by nature to do it any more than men are. Gender relations, feminists assert, are socially constructed just as are other institutions such as political and economic structures. Before the women's movement issues like family structure, sexuality (including sexual crimes) and domestic labour were seen as private issues and not open to the kind of discussion and debate that other social institutions were. The idea that the 'personal is political' revolutionized all this and set the stage for social change in our society.

The second claim, that 'sisterhood is powerful', had similar effects on society. It asserts that womanhood is the basis of a common oppression and a common struggle. In other words, society's definitions of womanhood and femininity dictated women's choices and experiences in society, rather than individual skills or preferences defining these choices and experiences. As a simple example, the prevailing concept of women's roles in the post World War II period meant that most women would marry, give up their careers/jobs and have children. In the words of one middle-aged Newfoundland woman I know, "It was just what you did." The idea that 'sisterhood is powerful' also called women to look outside their 'private' lives and relationships and seek change in a political alliance with other women. As a result, society has seen the emergence of women's centres (there are several in Newfoundland), feminist literature and a wide variety of women's groups. The effects of these developments on society, and on our lives as individuals, is profound and immeasurable. Perhaps that's a key reason why the women in Newfoundland fought so hard to keep their centres open in 1990.

Sociological terms

Grassroots—originating among or carried on by the "common people".

Lobby [*verb*]—to pressure decision-makers (e.g., politicians) to bring about change. (E.g., letter-writing, demonstrations)

Social movement—a group that is trying to change some or all aspects of society.

Politics—power relationships of all kinds.

Reading

This is democracy? Reflections on the occupation experience

T. MacKenzie

Well, it has been almost a year since our lives were turned upside down by the news of cuts in funding to the women's program. The 1.2 million dollar cut to women's centres across the country, which was announced in February of 1990, moved us to protest like we've never protested before. Hundreds of women and men were involved in months of protest that included a week long occupation of the Secretary of State offices in St. John's. This spurred women's groups across the country into similar actions. We've had a year to reflect on our struggle, and we're also now basking in the qualified glow of knowing that the funding (such as it is) has been reinstated, at least for now.

As I look back on that time, I realize that I have learned many lessons, but the thing that sticks with me is a new understanding and analysis of "democracy." I thought I knew what it was, and I

From *Waterlily*, Spring 1991, Volume 2, Number 4, p. 4.

Theresa MacKenzie was a board member of the St. John's Status of Women Council when the funding cuts were announced.

thought we (Canadians) had it. Well, they call it democracy, but for me it ends once you cast your vote. Some naive types (I refer mostly to myself here) were shocked and appalled by our inability to influence government decisions and policy. In retrospect, I think it was this very naiveté that enabled us to continue the fight, because if we had understood the true form that Canadian democracy takes we might have succumbed to helplessness and abandoned the fight much sooner. We had to believe that we could take on the government and win. I know I believed it (well...with slight wavering), and if I didn't I would not have stuck it out so long.

We are told that, in a democracy, every voice counts and that your voice will be, if not heeded, at least heard. We are told that there are legitimate and non-legitimate forms of protest—the legitimate including letter writing, lobbying, demonstrations, etc...We tried all those things, and even the most cynical amongst us were amazed that thousands of letters to the Secretary of State didn't warrant so much as a polite letter in response. I attended meetings with the Minister (*Ir*)Responsible for the Status of Women and with the Secretary of State, and quickly realized that these exercises were nothing more than a farce—they were clear attempts to silence and co-opt us. The concept of lobbying and meeting with these people seems pointless if you are not politically aligned with the government. Letter writing and postcard campaigns took up vast amounts of time, and had little real effect. I find this particular means of protest frustrating because it allows the politicians to deny the level of protest that exists, and it keeps us off the streets. I believe that we are encouraged to engage in this type of activity for these very reasons.

It became clear, as our frustrations mounted, that "legitimate protest" was silencing us instead of giving us a voice. One common response to this situation is paralysis and frustration. We did get frustrated in our efforts from time to time, but instead of becoming paralyzed by the so called political process, we strategized, planned and did what we knew we had to do—we occupied the offices of the Secretary of State. A strategy of exposure and embarrassment through non-violent action seemed to be the only logical route.

Occupations are not new, of course, but they were new to a lot of us. We really had little idea about how it would work, but it was clear that we had to take our actions a little further if we were to draw the attention of the general public, the media, and the politicians.

The general public was, in fact, the easiest to mobilize in this case. People were offended by the government's ability to find billions of dollars for defense while denying women's groups the comparatively paltry $1.6 million on which we depended. They became increasingly offended by the Tories' pathetic attempts at defending their action, which looked to many people like a brazen attempt to silence opposition. People who seldom explicitly supported us began to see things from our point of view, and many wrote letters and attended demonstrations on our behalf.

There were many lessons learned about the media as well. They were so important to our fight, yet it was extremely difficult to get coverage. We were told that ours was a regional story, for instance, and that we should so something slightly more extreme than an occupation if we expected to make news. Despite this, we knew that if the protest tactic was to draw attention and support to our issues, the media were essential to a positive outcome. A lot of the reporting that was done could be directly attributed to women and men in local and national media who made it an issue with their editors and producers, insisting that ours was an important story. Without them, it is unlikely that our story would have received the amount of attention it did, and we would have had difficulty in drawing support.

As for the government, it seems clear to me that they would have ignored our protests had we not been so effective at drawing attention to ourselves and to the issues. We exposed their weaknesses and related them to our strengths. We were also quite adept at pinpointing the contradictions in their policies, and I imagine we caused them significant discomfort and embarrassment. From the first day of the occupation, their discomfort was evident— there were meetings and frantic phone calls and the word from our friends on Parliament Hill was that we were a source of stress and worry for the Tories. What were they afraid of? We were peaceful and non-violent, and we assured them that we would not be destructive in any way. Yet we were carefully watched, followed, and bugged. The Tories were afraid of us because we posed as much of a threat to their interests as any violent or destructive group could—we threatened to expose them, to get people angry about their policies, to expose the inequalities that they institutionalized through their practices and programs, and to make such a noise about it that people would not forget at election time.

How did they deal with us? Their strategies included ignoring us, attempting to discredit us, calling in the police, and having us arrested. None of these strategies were particularly successful: they ignored us for a while but we wouldn't go away; we had built up such a high level of support and were so clear in talking about the situation that their attempts to discredit us were futile; when they finally called the police, and we left peacefully, they appeared desperate and bullying, and we won even greater public sympathy and support. Twenty-five of us did get arrested and were charged with public mischief; the charges were dropped after hanging over our heads for almost a year, but their attempts to intimidate us through the police did not work. We were not deterred from further action, and we knew that there were still others who were willing to be arrested for the cause.

I felt that many great things happened during that time of protest—I thank Brian et al. for helping us to strengthen our movement, and for increasing our popular support. I also feel that we've helped develop a popular movement, and stirred formerly non-active people into participation. The informal and formal coalitions that were generated in the course of the protest will probably be with us in future actions. I also think (hope) that we opened some eyes to the true nature of the "progressive" conservatives.

But despite our successes and the positive side-effects of our protests, I remain disgusted that so many people had to fight for two solid months, day and night, and through every possible channel, to get that relatively small amount of money returned to us. Many women put their lives on hold to try to get our funding back. The experience has made me look at the sorry state of the democratic process in this country, and has made me want to fight against it. In addition to ousting regressive and oppressive governments, I think we need to be putting energy into developing a democratic system that doesn't end at the polling booth, one that responds to the changing needs of the population, and one that doesn't ensure a virtual dictatorship to the elected government. We need government that is responsible and representative. Otherwise, we will continue to fight these small battles on a regular basis, and we will be less and less likely to win.

Lecture 2

'The protest line' in Burin—fighting government and business

The Government Game[10]

Come all you young fellows and list while I tell
Of the terrible misfortune that upon me befell.
Centralization they say was the name of the game.
But me I just calls it the government game.

My name it don't matter, I'm not young any more
But in all of my days I'd never been poor.
I'd lived a right good life and not felt no shame
Till they made me take part in the government game.

10 Song was composed by Newfoundland poet Al Pittman in collaboration with folksinger P.A. Byrne. Has been recorded on "Toward the Sunset", a Pigeon Inlet production. Reprinted with Author's permission.

My home was St. Kyran's a heavenly place;
It thrived on the fishing of a good hearty race.
But now it will never again be the same
Since they made it a pawn in the government game.

Sure the government paid us for moving away
And leaving our birthplace for a better day's pay.
They said that our poor lives would ne'er be the same
Once we took part in the government game.

It's not many years now since they all moved away
To places more prosperous way down in the bay.
There's not one soul left now, not one who remains;
They've all become part of the government game.

Now St. Kyran's lies there all empty as hell,
Except for the graveyards where our dead parents dwell.
The lives of their children are buried in shame,
They lost out while playing the government game.

To a place called Placentia some of them went
And in finding a new home their allowances spent.
So for jobs they went looking, but they looked all in vain
For the roof had caved in on the government game.

It's surely a sad sight, their moving around
Wishing they still lived by the cod fishing ground.
But there's no going back now, there's nothing to gain
Now that they've played in the government game.

They tell me our young ones the benefits will see
But I don't believe it, oh how can that be?
They'll never know nothing but sorrow and shame,
For their fathers were part of the government game.

And when my soul leaves me for the heavens above,
Take me back to St. Kyran's the place that I love.
And there on my gravestone, right next to my name,
Just say I died playing the government game.

We know that the definition of politics extends far beyond partisan politics and government. Sociologists and political scientists are concerned with all facets of power relationships, including protest and group dynamics, for example. Here we'll look at one particular social adaptation to economic instability and all it implies; the actual case study presented here is the protest line at the Burin fish plant in 1983 as documented by sociologist, Barbara Neis.

In the early 1980s, the 'Big Five' group of fish harvesting and processing companies suffered economic crumble and collapse, in varying degrees. Fish plants, the main and sometimes only employer in their respective communities were closed one after the other, in Ramea, Grand Bank, Fortune, Gaultois, Burin and elsewhere. The response differed from one community to another, illustrating the multiple political cultures on the island of Newfoundland. But, as Neis reports, the protest in Burin was "multi-faceted, collective and sustained".[11] In particular, it was a female-dominated activity.

So, what is a protest line? To a certain extent, it is self-explanatory but its definition needs some elaboration. First of all, protest lines are not union institutions; instead, they are established by community members *not* employed at the relevant worksite. Protest lines, unlike union demonstrations say, are not the actions of formally organized groups; it is working-class women, Neis says,

[11] Neis, in Sinclair, 1988, p. 139.

who are the backbone of protest lines in this province and elsewhere. Participants in a protest line walk back and forth across the entry to the plant. Their purpose is to give workers a legitimate excuse for not going to work. These workers may collect U.I. because they are not on strike. Thus, the operation of the plant is impaired and its employees do not have to resort to welfare (which is stigmatized in Newfoundland and other places).

The protest line in question was set up by an ad hoc group called the Burin Action Committee, itself a response to the threatened closure of Burin's only fish plant. (Like many Newfoundland fish plants, it was an economic mainstay of several surrounding communities, such as Lewin's Cove and Salt Pond, in addition to being the economic bedrock of historic Burin itself.) In November of 1982, Fishery Products closed the plant it had previously maintained was its most productive. By the end of February of 1983 the facility would be dismantled and all fish processing, consolidated in the larger centre of Marystown. Because of the economic importance of the Burin plant, coupled with the perceived lack of alternative economic opportunities, a social movement developed almost overnight.

Let's digress a little to clarify our understanding of social movements. Simply we may define them as collective attempts to change some or all aspects of society. Social movements, then, may be specific in their aims or general and comprehensive; they may be large- or small-scale; long-standing or short-term. One social scientist, David Aberle, has devised the following method of classifying social movements (this work was directed in particular at religious movements but it is of some use to us).

Diagram 1
Social movements

LOCUS OF CHANGE	SCOPE OF CHANGE: Total	SCOPE OF CHANGE: Partial
Individual	Redemptive (to help recover)	Alternative (to modify in part)
Whole society	Transformative (to change the form, essence or character of)	Reformative (to improve by removing faults and defects)

As an initial tactic the Burin Action Committee called for organized collective action at the level of the community. This included setting up a protest line, as had been done in Grand Bank the year before. The protest line operated in front of the fish plant for six months. Fairly secure economics allowed the line to last this long:[12]

> The protest line was intended to prevent trawlermen…from sailing in any of the nine trawlers that were tied to the wharf. It was also intended to stop the dismantling of the fish plant…and to serve as a source of media attention. The trawlers and the contents of the plant, including 700,000 lbs. of frozen processed fish, were held by the Burin Action Committee as collateral in the committee's confrontation with the company and the provincial and federal governments.

[12] Neis, p. 141, in Sinclair, 1988.

> Trawlermen respected the protest line, went home and applied for U.I. Plant workers soon followed. Both groups were able to draw U.I. so long as they did not participate in the protest line. This helped them endure months of deliberation by the company and the governments. The economic support provided by U.I. also helped ensure that plant workers would be less likely to undermine the protest by applying for...jobs...in Marystown.
>
> The date scheduled for dismantling the plant came and went.

The likelihood of some form of protest developing was certainly high. Neis focuses on the reasons why the protest line became a female political institution, especially the social and cultural roots of women's protest in Burin and elsewhere in outport culture.

First of all, Neis points out that some men did participate in the protest line but that their role was largely restricted to one of *support* (i.e,. keeping the fire going and other such duties). The sex-stratified nature of the protest line reflected the fact that women and men tend to participate in their own segregated organizations (such as the Kinsmen and Kinettes, the Lions and Lionesses).[13] There was also a sexual division of labour in the work activities of the area. In Neis' words:[14]

> In a community with a tradition of sex-segregation...it seems unlikely that a mixed-gender institution would have persisted in a context like the protest line where groups were small and people spent hours together...It would have been too awkward. The protest line had to be either male or female.

---

[13] The camaraderie that developed out of participation in these social groups was an "essential ingredient" to the continuance and success of the protest line.

[14] Neis, p. 144.

This point is central to Neis' findings.

The majority of the plant workers and trawlermen were male (they could not go on the protest line for fear of losing their entitlement to U.I.) Most of the protest line participants, then, were female relatives of plant workers, trawlermen and local store owners. But recruitment was also linked to kinship and/or friendship ties to other women. This kind of linkage was, according to Neis, the most important sort. We must take a closer look at women's political sculture in Burin to better understand why the protest line fitted into the realm of female activities. The following characteristics of women's political culture all contributed to the sustenance and eventual effectiveness of the Burin protest line:

1. the voluntary nature of the protest line which paralleled that of the various women's groups in the community;
2. women's fear that the plant closure would threaten family life (for example, trawlermen would be based in ports hundreds of miles away); and
3. women's experience with government bureaucracy (gained through dealing with U.I. in a seasonal economy).[15]

Women's groups and networks afforded their members some say in the way their communities' economic surplus was used. Through such groups women were also able to influence the cultural goals and values of their towns and outports. The protest line at the Burin fish plant was really a logical place for women to exercise their political concerns. In Burin the women were able to enjoy a measure of success; the plant was later re-opened for secondary fish processing although it did employ less people. The people of the region felt that the federal and provincial governments would likely have proceeded with the planned plant closure were it not for the protest line. The victory was encouraging because, as Neis points out, the women were able to use their latent power to achieve ends not normally in the realm of female political culture in rural Newfoundland.

---

[15] In addition to this last factor, I would add that traditionally in outport Newfoundland women had a high degree of control over the family economies. Undoubtedly, this is one of the factors at the root of women's involvement in the protest line.

References for Unit 2

- David F. Aberle. *The Peyote Religion Among the Navajo,* Chicago, Aldine, 1966.
- Nancy Adamson, Linda Briskin & Margaret McPhail. *Feminist Organizing for Change: The Contemporary Women's Movement in Canada,* Oxford University Press, Toronto, 1988.
- Bonnie S. Anderson & Judith P. Zinsser. *A History of Their Own: Women in Europe from Prehistory to the Present,* Volume II, Harper and Row, 1988.
- Rex Clark, ed. *Contrary Winds: Essays on Newfoundland Society in Crisis.* Breakwater, St. John's, 1986.
- *Encyclopedia of Newfoundland and Labrador,* Volume I and II.
- Erich Goode. *Collective Behaviour,* Harcourt Brace Jovanovich, New York, 1992.
- Maura Hanrahan. Lecture Notes, *Social Movements,* Sociology / Anthropology 3140, Memorial University, 1990–91.
- Ursula Kelly. *Marketing Place: Cultural Politics, Regionalism and Reading,* Fernwood, Halifax, 1993.
- Hilda Chaulk Murray. *More Than 50%: Woman's Life in a Newfoundland Outport, 1900–1950,* Breakwater, St. John's, 1979.
- Barbara Neis. "Doin' Time on the Protest Line: Women's Political Culture, Politics and Collective Action in Outport Newfoundland", pp. 133–153 in *A Question of Survival: The Fisheries and Newfoundland Society,* ed. by Peter R. Sinclair, ISER, 1988.
- John Porter. *The Vertical Mosaic: An Analysis of Social Class and Power in Canada,* University of Toronto Press, Toronto, 1968.

- Marilyn Porter. " 'A Tangly Bunch': The Political Culture of Outport Women in Newfoundland." Copyright Marilyn Porter, September, 1982. Published in *Newfoundland Studies,* Volume 1, No. 1, Spring, 1985, pp. 77-90.
- Vicky Randall. *Women and Politics,* St. Martin's Press, New York, 1982.
- Joseph R. Smallwood. *The Book of Newfoundland,* Volume I, 1972.
- Pauline Stockwood. *Mobilization of the Anti-Pornography Movement in Newfoundland (1983-1988): An Analysis of Ideology , Structure and Strategy,* Unpublished M.A. thesis, Dept. of Sociology, Memorial University, 1988.
- *Waterlily,* Vol. 2, No. 4, St. John's, 1991.

Unit Three

Social conflict and problems in Newfoundland

Lecture 1

Abuse by consensus

1979 was the "International year of the Child," announced by the United Nations to draw attention to the plight of the thousands of children who are homeless, hungry, ill, exploited as labourers, forced into prostitution, used as war pawns, and sexually and physically abused. 1979 was intended to promote research on exploited children and to recognize their right to a better way of life. In the Philippines, for example, child prostitution had become an important part of the national economy, particularly the tourism sector. The Marcos' government and local businesses allied together in their use of children for profit. Abuse takes place on several levels in this process: adults exploit children; men exploit women and children; the First (Western) World exploits the Third World; and the rich exploit the poor.

When we think of child sexual exploitation and abuse we have a tendency to think of poor countries like the Philippines, but our society is coming to a recognition that this sort of abuse occurs right here. Awareness is step one, as social activists would say, and we have barely begun to take this step. Recent social research indicates that child abuse is cross-cultural and, in western society, it is cross-class. Traditionally we have had a tendency to blame the victim in cases of incest, child battering and rape. It was often thought that the victim must have "done something" to deserve the abuse. Here in Newfoundland, as elsewhere, very often a blind eye was turned to situations of exploitation and abuse. This happened when female servants were raped by their well-off employers—such as happened in the Newfoundland novel *The Corrigan Women*—when young girls were forced to have sex with their fathers and uncles, and especially when men in positions of power abused children, as in the case of Roman Catholic priests in recent decades. Normally, the child, not the perpetrator, was stigmatized. In this section we will look at the Mount Cashel case which is unresolved at the time of writing but seems to be set to become one of the most horrific and large scale cases of sexual and physical abuse in Newfoundland's history. It may also serve as the impetus for social change.

The story of mistreatment of the boys at Mount Cashel Orphanage in St. John's is clearly an example of "abuse by consensus." This occurs when members of the community turn a blind eye or when they allow abuse to go on with their co-operation, often in the form of silence. According to Michael Harris,[1] over seventy people knew of the allegations of abuse made by the boys at the orphanage in the 1970s. These people were in positions of power; some worked for the Department of Social Services, others for the Justice Department, and some were members of the province's police force. There were some people who protested what was happening to Shane Earle and the other children: most notably Robert Hillyer of the Royal Newfoundland Constabulary and Ches Riche, a janitor at the residence. As we all now know, their voices and those of the boys were not heard.

The social analysis of what developed at Mount Cashel has not yet begun but we will take a few tentative steps toward an analysis in this lecture. The most important question for a social scientist involves 'why' a particular social problem occurs and is reproduced. Why did abuse by consensus develop amongst the community and throughout the decision-making centres in the province? A brief social history of the Catholic Church, especially the Irish Christian Brothers, provides us with the beginnings of answers to these questions.

---

1 See "Unholy Orders" by Michael Harris in *Through a Mirror Dimly*, our companion volume.

The Irish Christian Brothers in Newfoundland

The Irish Catholic who made their homes in Newfoundland were at a social and economic disadvantage from the beginning. Irish immigration began in the late 1700s with most immigrants coming from the southern Irish counties of Waterford and Wexford and the surrounding areas. In Newfoundland, the Catholics were subject to the same penal code that oppressed their kin in Ireland: they were fined for practicing their religion and for owning property. The backbone of the semi-underground culture was the priest who said mass in root cellars and other hiding places. With his religious activities outlawed, the priest was a fugitive. The dedication of the priest in such circumstances undoubtedly increased his prestige in the Irish Catholic community. Hence, the legacy of deferentialism of Newfoundlanders to religious (and political and other) officials was given one more opportunity to develop.

The Christian Brothers came to Newfoundland in 1875 by invitation to educate impoverished Catholic boys. In the strict sexual segregation of the Catholic Church, boys would be taught by male teachers, and girls by members of female religious orders (such as the Sisters of Mercy). It is undoubtedly true, too, that the education of girls in the 1800s was a less of a priority than the education of boys. When the Brothers came to teach in St. John's, students came from as far away as St. Mary's Bay. The Brothers were extremely educated and worldly by Newfoundland standards; as Michael Harris says, they must have made quite an impression on the community here. The Brothers aimed to offer the boys an education that would enable them to study at any well-established university. Many pupils, including working class boys, became part of Newfoundland's power elite in their positions as lawyers, merchants, politicians and priests.

Mount Cashel Orphanage itself was opened in 1898. It ran its own farm and offered trades training to residents, among other things. In that period of our history medical care was minimal and the death of one or both parents was not uncommon so the majority of the Brothers' charges were orphans. This had begun to change by the 1950s when the Department of Social Services got financially involved with Mount Cashel and began to place 'wards of the court' there. By this time medical care had improved so much that most children saw both parents survive well into their sixties and seventies. By the time the institution closed there were few, if any, orphans living there. The vast majority of the boys were of working class origins and from poverty-stricken homes: many were already victims of parental alcoholism, neglect or abuse in their families of origin.

The Mount Cashel legacy

By now, you may be coming up with ideas about why the abuse at Mount Cashel happened and why it went on unabated. I have already mentioned some reasons why priests and other religious figures met with such obsequious respect in Newfoundland. We saw that they kept underground religious practices alive in spite of the serious risks to their own lives. Secondly, officials like the Christian Brothers were much more educated than the general Newfoundland population. It seems that the Brothers have always been well respected and supported in the community. In one week during the depression they received over £30,000 in donations! Thirdly, in later years the orphanage was home to children from 'problem homes,' usually from the lower classes of society. In the words of Dereck O'Brien, "We were nobody, the scum of society. No one wanted us, nobody cared." It is true that, as anthropologists have found, physical and sexual abuse takes place in a wide range of cultures. Ours is no exception because of a variety of factors including religious oppression in Newfoundland, the class system inherent in our society and the social statuses and social power arrangements we have created. As someone who was raised as a Catholic, I also feel that the strict patriarchy of the church is to blame (women are still not allowed to serve as priests, for example). Sociologists and feminist scholars have shown that activities like violence are often highly valued in male-dominated institutions. For the boys at the Catholic school next to mine, getting hit by a Brother was merely part of going to school. The 'why' of child abuse may be hidden deep within the human psyche but the social environment we create can offer deterrents or permission. It seems that far too often Newfoundland society has given permission to abusers.

When we look at the Mount Cashel case, however, there are a number of promising developments. At the centre of these is the victim's action of violating society's unwritten rule, or norm, that "we do not talk about these things." Risking further opposition, hurt and increased stigmatization, the former residents of Mount Cashel sought justice for what had been done to them. In doing this, they helped to establish that the rights of victims have for too long been neglected. They also made it somewhat easier for other victims of child abuse, especially males, to come forward, and their case points out the problems associated with our class system and with our social power arrangements. Finally, the young men, through their honesty, showed us clearly how this sort of abuse is reproduced from one generation to another. Socialized into sexual and physical abuse, many of the boys became abusers themselves.

I'd like to end this lecture by pointing out that although this sensational case involves male children, female children are even more subject to sexual abuse. The national Badgely report found that one in four Canadian girls is the victim of rape or molestation.[2] Usually the perpetrator is someone well known to her and in a position of trust and power, such as her father, stepfather, grandfather, brother or uncle. It is still not unusual for members of the family to blame the victim or to tacitly co-operate in the abuse.

Sociological terms

Abuse by consensus—when abuse occurs with the stated or tacit approval of the community.

Patriarchy—the political/social structure which privileges men at the expense of women.

---

[2] The report estimated that one in ten boys is sexually abused although there is some evidence that this figure is higher and that boys have been more reluctant to come forward.

Lecture 2

The concept of the family

We have already mentioned the term 'socialization,' the process whereby a child gradually becomes a self-aware, knowledgeable person, skilled in the ways of the culture into which he or she is born. Through socialization each member of society learns the norms and values of the surrounding community. Socialization among our youngest members provides for 'social reproduction,' the process whereby patterns of behaviour are passed on from one generation to another. This enables societies to have structural continuity over time.

Before we go on with the discussion we need to be aware of some definitions. The 'family' is a group of people linked by kin connections with the adults assuming responsibility for the children. 'Kinship' ties are ties between individuals through marriage or blood relations (e.g., mother, siblings, etc.). 'Marriage' is a socially acknowledged and approved formal sexual union between two adults. The marriage bond makes the individuals kin to each other and to a wider group of kinspeople. This brings us to the 'extended family' which we may define as a multi-generational household of kinspeople. It may include grandparents, a married couple and their children. We can say the extended family exists also when the members are involved in a close or continuous relationship with one another (e.g., they may live in close proximity to one another and have economic ties). The 'nuclear family' consists of two adults, usually married to each other, living in the same household with their dependent (biological or adopted) children.

Forms of the family in Newfoundland

In Newfoundland the extended family has been an important institution. Traditionally, in our fishing communities brothers fished together (and still do in many cases) while their wives and children processed the fish onshore. Thus we can say that the family was an important economic unit. As in most industrialized (or semi- and post-industrialized) societies the family's role as an economic unit has declined. In Grand Falls, Windsor and Corner Brook, for instance, the family relies on outside labour relationships to produce and distribute the goods and services it needs. The husband may be employed at the mill while the wife may operate her own retail business downtown, for example. Economically, the family is much more dependent on and intertwined with the capitalist system. Consistent with this, many economic activities are carried out away from the home.

The form that Newfoundland families take is changing, too, as it is all across North America. Families are more mobile (i.e., apt to live in more than one community) these days. They are more likely to be nuclear families; in Labrador City and St. John's a large proportion of families live significant distances from their extended family members. Also, the proportion of single parent families is rising; these occur through divorce, having children outside marriage and, to a much lesser extent, the death of one parent. While family sizes have declined substantially in Newfoundland since Confederation, we still have the highest birth rate in Canada. The divorce rate here is very low and it seems that the extended family remains more important in Newfoundland than it does in many parts of Canada. Think about the reasons why this might be so.

It is safe to say that the importance of the family in this province has decreased somewhat in recent decades but it certainly doesn't appear that this social institution is a dying one. How many of your friends and acquaintances live in nuclear and extended families? The family is also the institution where 'basic socialization' (initial or foundation socialization of the child) takes place. Its importance has not changed in this respect, although, in many cases, daycare centres play a role in early socialization; this contrasts to early childhood development even a couple of decades ago.

In our culture the family is normally seen as a safe haven from the troubles of the world and a bedrock of support for individuals. This may be true for many cases but we as a society are becoming increasingly aware that the home is often the scene of social conflict, even violence, and other forms of abuse.

Sociological terms

Family—a group of people linked by kin connections and making up a household. Families may be **nuclear** (two adults and their dependent children) or **extended** (multi-generational). Both types exist in present-day Newfoundland.

Kinship—ties between individuals through marriage or blood relations.

Marriage—a socially approved formal sexual union between two adults.

Socialization—the process whereby an individual becomes skilled in the ways of her/his culture, and the roles she/he is expected to play.

Lecture 3

Family experiences through children's eyes

The family is central to the stories in many Newfoundland novels such as *House of Hate* (Percy Janes) and *january, february, june or july* (Helen Porter). While both the Stones and the Novaks are Newfoundland families, they are very different in form. Heather is from a single-parent family through divorce; she and her sisters have a half-sister they've never met living with their father in Iowa. All of the members of Heather's immediate family (those people she lives with) are female. The Novaks live in a working class neighbourhood in St. John's centre. The Stones live in industrialized Milltown and also are working class. Their family is male-dominated with the raging Saul as the father. The mother and daughter, Hilda, are very often the victims of sexist attitudes; witness Hilda's incessant, unpaid drudgery. Juju lives in a nuclear family (there seems to be no extended family around), which is quite traditional; the sexual division of labour reflects the usual pattern in Newfoundland families. The mother is responsible for cooking and cleaning at home while her husband earns his way at the mill and carries out "the outside work" on the house with his sons.

In modern Western society, including Newfoundland, we look to the family to fulfill our physical, emotional and social needs. In the media (e.g., TV's *The Cosby Show, Family Ties*) the family is seen as a haven; a safe, loving place for its members. We know from sociological, feminist and other research that this is very often not the case. In the last section we saw that many of the boys at Mount Cashel did not have their needs met in their families of origin. In Helen Porter's novel, Heather suffers from the abandonment of her father and a lack of attention from and communication with her mother and sisters. In Juju's case the problems are even more obvious; there are instances of physical abuse in the family and emotional battering is ongoing. Percy Janes is careful to show how Saul is the child of his own early family circumstances, including poverty and neglect. Near the end of the novel, Juju remembers his troubled father:[3]

> Poverty, and its Siamese twin ignorance, must have caused him endless humiliations of spirit long before he was a man, and bred in him that profound modesty which is such a distinguishing mark of our people as a whole that it amounts to an island-wide inferiority complex. Emotional constriction—and from such causes—has always been a well-known feature of Newfoundland life. It was as though all the hardship and hunger our fathers collectively endured had materialized in the form of a spectre which dogged them all through their days and was forever warning them to put no trust in this life nor in anyone connected with it or with them for as long as life endured.

Juju is acutely aware of the process and effects of socialization. Of his brothers (as adults) he writes:[4]

> It seemed that in childhood they had been inoculated with a virus which broke out later in the form of an almost complete paralysis of the human being. Neither Ank, Racer, Crawfie, nor Fudge could shake free of the strange fatal lethargy which the spewing forth of a father's indiscriminate hate had cast over the will of each one of them.

3 Janes, p. 319.

4 Janes, p. 320.

Not surprisingly several of Juju's brothers had developed drinking problems and were abusive to their own children.

Newfoundland is certainly not the only society to suffer the effects of 'dysfunctionalism' in the family. And there is a real dearth of social science research into the family in our province. We cannot at this point say that the Newfoundland family has more of a tendency toward dysfunctionalism than families elsewhere in the Western world. Nor can we say with confidence at this point that there is a prototypical Newfoundland family. What we can say is that we have in common with other societies many of the social problems that are documented. We do know that Newfoundlanders drink more alcohol per capita than residents of almost every other province. It is likely, then, that there is more alcoholism in the family here than in most places in Canada. I think that it is also safe to conclude, as Percy Janes does, that poverty and economic instability have played a significant role in the development of dysfunctional families like the Stones. In the words of one of our ballads:

The best thing to do is to work with a will;
For when 'tis all finished you're hauled on the hill,
You're hauled on the hill and put down in the cold,
And when 'tis all finished you're still in the hole,
And it's hard, hard times.

Fatalism and social deference have for a long time been characteristics widespread in the Newfoundland community. At the end of his story, Juju points optimistically to Confederation with Canada as a way out of Newfoundland's poverty and hardship. You may want to consider how accurate his view was in light of the past forty-odd years of union with Canada.

For our discussion of the family I have relied on Newfoundland fiction or literature as well as personal observations as a sociologist and a member of the society. There is a wealth of fictional accounts that provide us with insights into family relationships in Newfoundland, which you may want to read. These include *The Story of Bobby O'Malley, The Time of Their Lives, The Divine Ryans* (all by Wayne Johnston) and *The Corrigan Women* (by M.T. Dohaney). Despite the lack of social science studies on the family in

Newfoundland, there are some books which are useful. In *Cat Harbour: A Newfoundland Fishing Settlement,* James Faris gives an anthropological account of how behavioural norms are generated and coded in one outport. Kinship relationships are also studied in Melvin Firestone's book, *Brothers and Rivals: Patrilocality in Savage Cove.* In this outport the patrilocal extended family (i.e., the married couple lives in the locality associated with the husband's father's relatives) is the most important social unit. Firestone looks at how fishing families in Savage Cove construct their social relationship around egalitarianism and competition. (This may look contradictory at first.) Firestone's research shows us just how much the family was valued in outport Newfoundland.

Reading

Profile: Never despair is author's message in novel

by Nina Patey
Express Columnist

In 1970 a book was published about the inner workings of a family in rural Newfoundland during the 1940s and 50s. It takes in the period of Newfoundland history from 1900–63, the first 45 years at least being the hardest in living memory for eking out a living in this place. Undoubtedly it was worse between 1600 and 1900—three hundred years of shipwrecks, starvation, impoverishment and subservience. Minus the shipwrecks, they're the conditions facing most of the world's population today—the Third World.

The book was born out of these centuries of hardship. The consequences for a man's life who was conceived in poverty and raised in destitution.

The author was Percy Janes and the book was *House of Hate*.

"Many see the book as a gigantic put down of Newfoundland. Others do not. They will tell me, 'Yes, that's exactly what life was like'."

We in Newfoundland look at ourselves as having a strength of character born out of the hardship of living in this place. Percy Janes

From *The Express*, February 26, 1992, pp. 26–27. Published by *The Express*, St. John's, Nfld. Reprinted by permission.

saw not the generosity, tolerance and sense of humour which can come from such roots but the brutishness, hypocrisy and cruelty which can also be the fruits of a life of drudgery.

The book's principal character is the father Saul. It is from him that all else flows. His wife starts out a strong, independent minded woman who had cooked for the construction workers during the beginnings of a pulp and paper mill (Corner Brook). After 50 years of marriage to Saul, she is a desperate, embittered, exhausted person trying to keep it all together. Saul's offspring bear childhood scars for life.

Out of reach language

The book uses the language I could hear growing up in Bonavista Bay when I was beyond the reach of my parents and the Salvation Army barracks.

"Be the lard Jes'," etc., etc.

This book explains a lot about the rural Newfoundland of the past and even of the more recent 1960s—the still too-large families, where if some of the kids got fed and clothed that was as much as their families could manage; the predominance of liquor in the lives of the men or boys over 15, the coarseness of the language, the flourishing, unbounded sexism implicit in the 14-year-old male who would say, "Mudder git me anudder cup o' tea."

This is a side of rural Newfoundland that we do not talk about. We prefer to wax eloquent about blueberry picking, scenic drives, beaches and ponds, playing in the woods, climbing trees and rocks, paddling in the salt water, bonfire night and mummering.

Other things, though, could be seen, and heard and smelt. The stench of outhouses, of kitchens stuffy and uncleaned. The obesity of women from too many potatoes, too much depression and not enough fruit, vegetables and respect. The emaciated little girl in Grade 3, unkempt, unwashed, uncared for by an exhausted mother pregnant yet again and living in a cold hovel near a bog.

"I have received letters and calls over the years. One woman said that she was married to her husband for 25 years and never really understood him until she read that book. It is about an era. Class was very important, it is about life among the working people of that era. Work was the law of life."

We talked about this harshness, the belt, the rules, the work ethic, the bareness of life, the lack of humour or appreciation of anything refined, the suffocating practicality.

No purpose

"My maternal grandmother was an extreme case of total lack of imagination. She saw no purpose in writing something, unless A, it was true and B, it had a moral. They were kind of narrow and kind of fierce."

I was trying to understand what kind of life Saul's mother was able to give him if she had survived a shipwreck, had several children to provide for. "Would she have gone to work for someone—as a 'girl' they were called—even if they were middle-aged women? Would someone have taken her in? How bereft of affection was he in childhood that he had nothing in him on which to build a relationship of trust or love with his own children, much less his wife? Had his mother beat him?"

He was worn out with work. They were probably given a shack to live in. She lived in that little cove—Spencer's Cove in Conception Bay, all her life—and hardly ever left it."

Percy Janes was living in England when he wrote *House of Hate*.

"There I could be psychologically freer. This is a common experience of writers, particularly for their first novel. If you stay in the same place you are so much in the toils of the experience that you need to get away so that you can be free to use it as material for fiction."

The character Saul, who is based on the author's father, is an only child and lives a destitute life in Raggety Cove (Spencer's Cove) at the beginning of this century. But in reality there were other brothers and sisters. This was worse than being an only child, since as the eldest he had responsibility for the younger children to go out to work, even as a child."

"There was no milk. He lived on fish and bread. He never tasted an orange until he was a young man. He was six or seven years old out turning fish all day. Hauling turns of water. He never had a day in school."

"My father had gone from nothing to having a good job in the mill— well—good money. He thought we never appreciated it. And we didn't. I think most kids take what their parents have for granted—as a given. He thought we did not respect him because he could not read or write. He was afraid that we would try to fool him."

Drinking as rite

In successive generations there was the same narrowness without the moral pressure of the work ethic or religion. "If you didn't drink by a certain age you weren't really a man, it was a rite of passage. But it was not a good thing, it was very destructive."

"Where in England did you write *House of Hate*?" I asked.

"Mostly in London. Believe it or not I wrote it all out in long hand. I typed it. Revised it, and typed it again. It was 310 pages. It is the third version that circulated to the publishers."

It went to agents and publishers in the States and England and was rejected three times. When it was accepted for publication by McClelland and Stewart, Jack McClelland sent him a telegram—not a letter—of acceptance.

"You can imagine that was a great day for me. So I had to suffer those rejections before I could get going as a writer at all."

Margaret Laurence wrote the preface to Janes' book. He had met the Manitoba-born writer in the early 1970s when they were introduced through mutual friends in England. Later he was a paying guest at her home in Buckinghamshire for a year.

"I didn't have any knowledge of this beforehand. It was a pleasant surprise. I had good luck with that book. Two highly reputed Canadian authors took part in its getting published." Farley Mowat was a friend of Jack McClelland's and a reader for McClelland and Stewart. He gave the book a good recommendation.

"I got the proofs and corrected them." *House of Hate* came out in hard cover and was pretty well received. "It wasn't what you call a seller but it has sold steadily for 21 years." There have been several editions in soft cover and in 1991 the novel was turned over to Breakwater Books who will be bringing out a new edition this year.

"I was 48 years old and as yet unpublished or only obscurely so you can imagine my frame of mind."

Traveller, not tourist

The story has never been turned into a play although two attempts have been made: one by Paul O'Neil and the other by Rising Tide Theatre with direction by Donna Butt.

"It would make a great film," I said.

"You would not have to write much screen play because there is a lot of dialogue," he said.

I think it would be like those heavy Scandinavian films with Ingrid Bergman and Liv Ullmann.

Janes lived in England for 12 years—in London mostly. This was the base from which he took trips around the British Isles to Sussex, Scotland, Dublin, and, at different periods to France, Germany, Belgium, Austria, Spain, and Gibraltar.

"I travelled on a shoe string. I was a traveller not a tourist."

Travelling in North and Central America has also been a part of Janes' lifestyle as a writer and traveller.

"I've gone across country two or three times, to the States, Mexico and Costa Rica, spending winters in Mexico and Costa Rica."

Janes has written four novels, a novella, a book of short stories and a book of poetry.

"In the meantime, I continue to write. A life of 21 years is not so bad for a novel. I guess the moral is 'Never despair.' I'm hoping the novel will go on under Clyde Rose but that remains to be seen."

He is observant of the changes that time has brought to the health of Newfoundlanders.

"Children now are better grown. The children I see on the bus now have nice teeth. The children in Newfoundland used to be rickety looking, with rotting teeth and half-nourished. They almost looked like freaks. Many people do not know how far we were behind the rest of Canada."

"My family regarded my desire to be a writer as foolishness, that is the word that was used. 'That's only old foolishness. You're gonna become a bad case'. I don't regret it, Nina, if I'd gone another way, if I had gone to work in the mill, I would have perished."

Lecture 4

Women and the family in Newfoundland

As we examine the role of women in the family, I will rely on two academic publications, as well as my own observations. The first of these accounts is by folklorist Hilda Murray Chaulk: Chapter 5, "The Woman and Her Family: Pregnancy, Childbirth and Infant Care" in *More than 50%* (1979). The other is by sociologist/anthropologist Dona Lee Davis: "'Shore Skippers' and 'Grass Widows': Active and Passive Women's Roles in a Newfoundland Fishery" in *To Work and to Weep: Women in Fishing Economics,* Nadel-Klein and Davis (1988).

Grey Rock Harbour women

In Grey Rock Harbour on the south coast of the island, where Davis carried out her fieldwork, women fit into one of two categories: 'shore skippers' or 'grass widows.' The latter are more common and more favourably viewed than the role of shore skipper. Grass widows are involved in their husbands' fishing work in both emotional and more obviously practical ways. The grass widow is greatly admired for her role as a successful organizer, nurturer and family manager. Her role is seen as the proper female one; it is synonymous with female dignity. As part of this role, women are expected to be competent, yet self-effacing. We've all seen our mothers and grandmothers minimize their abilities and accomplishments both inside and outside the home! The other female role, that of shore skipper, is envied but not honoured. Shore skippers are seen as an interference in the men's fishing business. They have an alleged attitude of superiority; they are ambitious and thus challenge the traditional egalitarian ethic of rural Newfoundland. Impression management is crucial here. And a women's self-esteem and social status will be greatly influenced by the way she is seen by others.

Unfortunately, there has been little written on women in this province. (We can also see this as an opportunity.) Davis' fieldwork and the analysis she offers lead us to ask a number of sociological questions. For example, how fixed or prescribed are women's roles in Newfoundland? And men's roles? Was personal choice a familiar or alien concept in rural Newfoundland, historically and in the present day? What kind of recognition was afforded to women in Newfoundland communities? And to their work? There are dozens, even hundreds, of songs, poems and stories honouring the contribution men have made to Newfoundland society ("The Badger Drive" and "Let Me Fish Off Cape St. Mary's" are examples of such folksongs). But it seems that there are few examples of women's work getting the recognition it deserves. Let's look at the kind of life a woman led in outport Newfoundland in the first half of this century.

Elliston women

In Elliston, Bonavista Bay, earlier in this century, motherhood was considered a woman's central role. A woman would be expected to conceive within a year of her marriage, but pregnancy was not discussed as openly as it is today. Hilda Chaulk Murray reports that a married woman was said to be "in the family way" or "that way again, you know." Unmarried women were said to be "knocked up" or "in trouble" while their children were known as "merry-begots." Although there are horrific stories about the plight of unwed mothers in our history, generally speaking they were not discriminated against. Children born out of wedlock were reared by the mother's parents as their own offspring or by the mother herself and her husband, who might or might not be the father.

In Elliston, there were a host of rules and standards surrounding pregnancy. For example, a pregnant woman was not supposed to deliberately smell anything and her cravings had to be satisfied or the child would be born with birthmarks. If a woman gave birth to a crippled or deformed child, it was said that she had mocked such a child. The community strongly believed that the actions, desires and conduct of a pregnant woman would affect her baby. Some sociologists would argue that all of these rules and taboos served as a means of controlling a woman's behaviour in a patriarchal society, such as existed in Newfoundland.

In the Elliston area, as in many other parts of Newfoundland, birth control was not used in the first half of the century. According to Murray, it was not uncommon for a family to have a dozen or more children but, by the 1950s, large families had become more uncommon. Traditionally, babies would be born to a couple every two years and this was seen as "the Lord's will." The newborn child added to the workload of the mother and the older girls in the family. Girls assumed responsibilities at an early age to prepare them for their future role in the community.

As in most regions of rural Newfoundland, "borning babies" was considered to be women's work. In Elliston, men were not even allowed in the house while a woman was delivering a baby. Men's work in this area was restricted to fetching the midwife and transporting her to the expectant mother on time. The midwife would travel, depending on the season and region in which she worked, by dog sled, boat, horse and sleigh, or horse and buggy. Sometimes she would have to travel during blizzards, and often by foot, several miles or more. Doctors were called in only for emergencies, however, and for many places doctors were completely inaccessible. My great-aunt Rachel Hanrahan Abbott (1890–1986) gave birth to thirteen children (of whom eight survived) and she did not come into contact with a doctor until she was an old woman. She never visited a hospital in her life. Aunt Rachel's situation was far from unusual. Untold numbers of Newfoundland women died in childbirth; even today about two a year do not survive giving birth.

During the birth the other children would often be sent to stay with neighbours or relatives. In Elliston, children were not told the biological facts about pregnancy and childbirth; instead, they were told that babies came from the midwife's black bag or the cellar.

Elliston women had two customs pertaining to the mother's recovery from the birth; both of these have since died out, Murray reports. These are "Up-sitting Day" and "the Groaning Cake." Normally a new mother would stay in bed for ten days but this varied; it might be longer with the first child and shorter if the woman's services were badly needed. The tenth day after the birth was called "Up-sitting Day" and the midwife and the local women, especially those who had been at the birth, would gather at the mother's house for a cup of tea. At this time they would share a special cake called the "Groaning Cake," which was usually out of the ordinary but sometimes only raisin bread, depending on family economics. A more modern tradition in Newfoundland is the baby shower, held by the pregnant woman's female friends and relatives before the baby's birth. During the shower the expectant mother is given gifts, like clothing and diapers, for the baby and the group shares refreshments and may play bingo or card games for prizes. The "Groaning Cake" is said to be a derivative of an English custom while baby showers are more North American. But not very much is known about the origins of these traditions. It is only recently in our history/herstory that the family is seen as a valid subject of study for scholars.

References for Unit 3

- Leslie Bella. *The Christmas Imperative: Leisure, Family and Women's Work,* Fernwood, Halifax, 1992.
- Cecilia Benoit. *Midwives in Passage: The Modernization of Maternity Care,* ISER, MUN, 1991.
- Dona Lee Davis. *Blood and Nerves: An Ethnographic Focus on Menopause,* ISER, MUN, 1983.
- Paul S. Dinham. *You Never Know What They Might Do: Mental Illness in Outport Newfoundland,* ISER, MUN, 1977.
- M.T. Dohaney. *The Corrigan Women,* Ragweed Press, Charlottetown, 1988.
- James Faris. *Cat Harbour: A Newfoundland Fishing Settlement,* ISER, MUN, St. John's, 1972.
- Alison Feder. *Margaret Duley: Newfoundland Novelist, a Biographical and Critical Study,* Harry Cuff, St. John's, 1983.
- Lawrence Felt. " 'Take the Bloods of Bitches to the Gallows': Cultural and Structural Constraints upon Interpersonal Violence in Rual Newfoundland", ISER, MUN, 1987.
- Melvin M. Firestone. *Brothers and Rivals: Patrilocality in Savage Cove,* ISER, MUN, St. John's, 1980.
- Harold Harwood. *Tomorrow will be Sunday,* Paperjacks, Don Mills, Ontario, 1975.
- Michael Harris. *Unholy Orders: Tragedy at Mount Cashel,* Viking, Markham, Ontario, 1990.
- William A. Haviland. *Anthropology,* Holt, Rinehart & Winston, Inc., Toronto, 1991.

- Percy Janes. *House of Hate,* McClelland & Stewart, Toronto, 1970.
- Michael Mitterauer and Reinhard Sieder. *The European Family,* Basil Blackwell, Oxford, 1982.
- Dereck O'Brien. *Suffer Little Children: The Autobiography of a Foster Child,* Breakwater, 1991.
- Patrick O'Flaherty. *The Rock Observed: Studies in the Literature of Newfoundland,* University of Toronto Press, Toronto, 1979.
- Hilda Chaulk Murray. *More Than 50%: Woman's Life in a Newfoundland Outport, 1900–1950,* Breakwater, St. John's, 1979.
- Jane Nadel-Klein and Dona Lee Davis, eds. *To Work and to Weep: Women in Fishing Economies,* ISER, 1988.
- Linda Ann Parsons. *Passing the Time: The Lives of Women in a Northern Industrial Town,* Unpublished M.A. thesis, Sept. of Sociology, Memorial University, 1987.
- Helen Porter. *january, february, june or july,* Breakwater, St. John's, 1988.
- Anuradha Vittachi. *Stolen Childhood: In Search of the Rights of the Child,* Polity Press, Cambridge, UK, 1989.
- John Widdowson. *If You Don't Be Good: Verbal Social Control in Newfoundland,* ISER, MUN, 1977.

Unit Four

Work and development in Newfoundland

Lecture 1

Industrialization in Newfoundland

The aim of this lecture is to provide an overview (emphasizing, again, one sociologist's opinions) about the process of industrialization as we have seen it operate in Newfoundland. We will look at government policies regarding industrial development and at the effects that they have had on society and culture. You may be thinking that Newfoundland is not an urban-industrial society and, of course, for the most part you are right. But let's think about this for a moment. The pulp and paper industry is the engine of communities like Grand Falls-Windsor and Corner Brook. The iron mines on Bell Island operated for about sixty years and served as the financial bedrock of Newfoundland for much of this time. (During the most active days of the mine the island had a population of 18,000, second only in size to St. John's.) There have been long-term miners in communities such as Buchans and more on-again, off-again mining activities carried out in St. Lawrence and other Newfoundland towns.

Industrial development was the *raison d'être* of most of the inland settlements (Grand Falls-Windsor, for example) and it has shaped the lives of many thousands of people in this province. An example of this is a very moving video called "Our Hometown" made by the Buchans Youth Committee in the early 1980s. In this video, the high school students expressed their strong feelings for their economically threatened community (the mines were about to close) and articulated their wish to keep Buchans viable. Speaking from my own experience, while teaching at MUN, I have had a large number of students whose lives as Newfoundlanders have revolved around the paper, mining, or other industries, rather than the fisheries, which is, of course, inextricably linked with Newfoundland society and culture. Their lives are a valid part of Newfoundland society and culture, too, but very often Newfoundlanders and observers of the culture have restricted their focus to exclude non-fishing people. This point is addressed in the folksong, "The Badger Drive," which you can find at the end of this lecture. The song points out that loggers have not been celebrated as much as fishermen have; this is true of women, as well, who have largely been omitted from Newfoundland history and social sciences. This can be seen, for example, in the physical representations of our culture—souvenirs, for instance, invariably relate to the fishing industry. It is virtually impossible to overstate the importance of the fishery to the development of Newfoundland society. But let's not do this to the exclusion of other aspects of life on the island. This section of the book is an attempt to redress the imbalance and explore sociologically a part of the society and culture that has been somewhat neglected.

Industry and government policies in Newfoundland

The government of Canada has traditionally been active in society and economy; it has played a significant role in shaping both provincial and national economies. In 1949, the new province of Newfoundland, with its problems of economic uncertainty, became the object of an onslaught coming from both Ottawa and St. John's. In this section we'll look at the types of policies that were advocated and the kinds of results they had. Although it is very summary in form, we can say that so far there have been two distinctive phases in industrial development in post-Confederation Canada: the urban-industrial phase and the government dependency phase. The first of these is characterized, briefly, by the establishment of a variety of mega-projects such as the Stephenville linerboard mill. The second is characterized by the proliferation of government sponsored make-work projects, particularly throughout rural Newfoundland. My position is that neither of these approaches to social and economic development is appropriate or beneficial to our communities. To put it colloquially, we kind of fell into each of these stages; neither was the result of careful study and planning and neither were developed to suit the strengths, weaknesses and peculiarities of Newfoundland economy and society.

Growth pole philosophy and the urban-industrial phase

Following Confederation in 1949, both the federal and provincial governments aimed to industrialize what was probably Canada's least industrial region. Because this process required the provision of infrastructure many wage jobs were created (particularly for men, who went to work building roads, schools, hospitals, and public buildings).[1] Accordingly, during the 1950s and 60s, a variety of large-scale, *capital-intensive* (rather than labour-intensive) projects were developed throughout the province, including Labrador.[2] These projects included the Stephenville linerboard mill, the oil refinery at Come-By-Chance, iron ore mines in Labrador (which many islanders worked in) and other mega-projects. Both the federal and provincial governments favoured and promoted this sort of urban-industrial development for Newfoundland. Phrases like "the new Newfoundland" came into common usage and many of you are no doubt aware that then-Premier Smallwood is alleged to have told fishermen "burn your boats, there'll be two jobs for every man." For politicians and workers alike, a break with the economic uncertainties of the past was imminent. Looking back at that era, many social scientists are quite cynical about the attempts to industrialize

---

1 Newfoundland had witnessed only one such widespread opportunity for paid employment once before: during World War II when thousands of men and women earned relatively large salaries at the U.S. military bases scattered around the island (at St. John's, Argentia, Gander and Stephenville).

2 Capital-intensive means utilizing a large proportion of financial resources as opposed to using a large proportion of human resources (i.e. labour-intensive). The latter creates more jobs.

Newfoundland; many of us are acutely aware that, for a whole host of reasons, Newfoundland will never become a miniature Southern Ontario centre of manufacturing. We are also more *culturally sensitive,* perhaps, than society was then; that is, now we can see an inherent value in traditional Newfoundland ways of life and we no longer view the urban-industrial way of life as the only or even most valid one.[3] Common knowledge holds that hindsight is a wonderful thing and this is true for social scientists to be sure. Let's look briefly at why our leaders felt it necessary to transform Newfoundland into a different place.

From the 1950s onwards, economists and other social scientists, such as geographers, all over the western world enthusiastically promoted something called "growth pole philosophy" (or GPP). Basically, GPP held that it was important for regions to have dominant centres or growth poles in which industry and commerce would be concentrated. These cities would serve as a spring-board for economic development by attracting the brains and talent of the area and becoming centres for innovation. The flipside of GPP was that without a growth pole, a region was doomed to economic stagnation and even depression. The rationale behind the philosophy was that "...growth does not appear everywhere all at once: it appears in points or growth poles with varying intensity..."[4] The resettlement programs that we look at shortly were efforts to harness and promote economic development in this manner, by establishing "dominant nodes" or growth centres. To summarize, the arguments put forward for growth centres in general (and for resettlement in Newfoundland in particular) are:

1. it is more efficient to concentrate infrastructure;
2. innovation is at the root of development and it is more likely to occur in larger towns;
3. larger centres are needed to get quality support services; and
4. it is politically necessary to spread development to distressed regions and this can be done through the promotion of growth poles.

---

3 That is not to say that our society and culture are free of problems as we saw in the last unit.

4 Moseley, 1974, p. 4, cited Perroux, 1964, p. 143.

You may be aware of other reasons cited for greater spatial concentration and many of them contain, at least on the surface, a grain of truth. However, there is evidence that growth poles generally succeed at the expense of less favoured areas. Another reason why GPP may not be appropriate in the Newfoundland case is that the population is too small, even after resettlement, to become a success along the lines of the urban-industrial success.[5] I contend that other forms of development are more suitable for Newfoundland and we'll examine some of these later.

What follows is the song "The Badger Drive." It can provide us with insights into work and technology, employee-labour relations in Newfoundland logging and the Newfoundland working-class culture (although one song could by no means provide a complete picture).

The Badger Drive[6]

There is one class of men in this country that never is mentioned by song,
And now since their trade is advancing they'll come out on top before long.
They say that our sailors have danger, and likewise our warriors bold,
But there's none know the life of a driver what he suffers with hardship and cold.

Chorus

With their pike-poles and pevies and bateaus and all,
And they're sure to drive out in the spring that's the time.

---

5 This is not the only reason, of course. Another problem is that Newfoundland is too distant from major markets; this is relevant to the manufacturing of some products. There is a growing body of socio-economic literature available on development in Newfoundland.

6 From *The Old Time Songs and Poetry of Newfoundland: Songs of Folklore, Humour, Tragedy, and History from the Days of our Forefathers*, 1926, p. 17 by Mr. John V. Devine. Published by Gerald S. Doyle Ltd.

With the caulks in their boots when they get on the logs
And it's hard to get over their time.

Billey Dorothey he is the Manager and he's a good man at the trade,
And when he's around seeking drivers he's like a train going down grade,
But still he is a man that's kind hearted, on his word you can always depend,
And there's never a man that works with him but likes to go with him again.

I tell you to-day home in London, "The Times" it is read by each man,
But little they think of the fellows that drove the wood on "Mary Ann,"
For paper is made out of pulpwood and many more things you may know,
And long may they live to drive it upon "Paymeoch" and "Tomjoe."

The drive it is just below Badger and everything is working grand,
With a jolly good crew of picked drivers and Ronald Kelley in command,
For Ronald is boss on the river and I tell you he's a man that's alive,
He drove the wood off Victoria, now he's out on the main River Drive.

So now to conclude and to finish I hope that ye all will agree,
In wishing success to all Badger and the A.N.D. Company,
And long may they live for to flourish and continue to chop drive and roll,
And long may the business be managed by Mr. Dorothey and Mr. Cole.

Sociological terms

Capital-intensive—when an industry or enterprise requires a large amount of financial resources, we say it is capital-intensive. (E.g., oil industry)

Labour-intensive—when labour is a more necessary ingredient than capital, an industry or enterprise is labour-intensive. (E.g., inshore fishery)

Growth pole philosophy—Popular during the 1950s and 1960s. It held that growth centres (i.e., industrial/commercial conurbation) were needed for development to occur.

Lecture 2

Resettlement in Newfoundland

The resettlement programs show beyond doubt that both Ottawa and St. John's (i.e., the federal and provincial governments) were committed to transforming Newfoundland society and economy along the lines of the urban-industrial growth model that had worked, at least for some time, in Central Canada, Australia and Britain. The resettlement programs were carried out over the two and a half decades following Confederation. They resulted in the evacuation of several hundred communities which had an average population of sixty-five.[7] Some areas of the province were more transformed than others; Placentia Bay, Newfoundland's largest bay, was decimated by resettlement, particularly the once-populated islands like Oderin and Red Island. Not all of the evacuated communities were as small as the average, however; some were fairly large by Newfoundland standards. Others, like Ireland's Eye in Trinity Bay, had traditionally enjoyed economic prosperity and were viable outports.

Ostensibly, the Canadian and Newfoundland governments used resettlement to centralize economic production. Other related reasons cited were improved opportunities in education, more available health care and easier (i.e., road) transportation. One researcher told me, in an unconfirmed verbal report, that the

---

7 Rowe, 1980, p. 520.

Newfoundland government was also concerned about inbreeding in some of the smallest, most isolated outports, and wished to prevent inbreeding in the future. It is quite possible that this was on government's agenda but it would have been undiplomatic and therefore unwise to make it public. The stated purpose of the program, then, was to bring people in isolated regions closer to modern conveniences and to decrease the dispersion of the province's population.

Still, the resettlement programs of both governments were ad hoc, rather than well-planned and organized. To observers and participants there seemed to be very little common sense behind the plans; in a few cases, such as the tiny villages near Carbonear, Conception Bay, people were moved only a few miles down the road, while some of the most isolated outports were not even included in the program. The resettlement schemes operated by offering financial incentives to people of earmarked communities to move to larger centres like Marystown, Grand Bank and others. Note that the population in Newfoundland was so dispersed that even these "growth poles" had only several thousand people each, if that; hardly enough to make them urban-industrial centres. In the early lectures we discussed how the fishery was the original reason for European settlement in Newfoundland; our settlement patterns were (or are) a perfect adaptation to an inshore fishery-based economy. Not surprisingly, it is very difficult to convert this socio-economic system into an industrial, capitalist one.

I am sure that many of the students of Newfoundland society are familiar with the social and emotional costs of resettlement. I remember my Uncle Mike Bruce telling me stories of how old men from the Placentia Bay islands sat on the Placentia wharves and cried for what they had lost. Many families sold or left behind their houses, boats and livestock; some of them became part of the long-term unemployed because of the job shortages that have plagued Newfoundland. The popular recording artists Simani summed it up well in one of their songs called "Outport People" in which an elderly resettled man reminisces about his former home. On the other hand the children of the resettled people were able to avail of medical assistance and educational opportunities their parents had lacked.

From Bragg's Island to Gambo

You may have seen the Land and Sea program about an older couple who resettled from one of the Bonavista Bay islands to the town of Gambo. Or you may have seen David Blackwood's etchings immortalizing the fishing families leaving Bragg's Island in their boats, forever. Researchers Noel Iverson and Ralph Matthews report in a 1968 paper (written during the last days of the resettlement era) that in 1945 Bragg's Island had a population of 231, nearby Deer Island, 102, and Green's Island, 70. For the next five years the population of the islands remained stable but by 1954, these settlements were nearly deserted.

Before we return to the specifics of Bragg's Island, it is interesting to ponder the question, 'how small does a community have to be before its residents decide it's no longer feasible to live there'? In their research, Iverson and Matthews found that there was no clear answer to this question: the people of Bragg's Island decided to resettle after their numbers dwindled to sixty families; some residents of Ireland's Eye, Trinity Bay, stayed until there were only seven families left. There are other oddly contradictory examples on record as well. In fact, much of the available evidence indicates that social patterns are difficult to detect in the resettlement period in Newfoundland. Another often asked question is 'how isolated does a community have to be for it to be considered for resettlement'? Again, there is very little sense of uniformity in this regard: witness the example of Freshwater (very near Carbonear), a tiny village that became part of the resettlement program. Yet Iverson and Matthews make the intriguing but sensible point that it is those communities on the periphery of developing areas that have the greatest tendency to resettle, *not* the most isolated outports. This would suggest that contact with other, larger towns may be a factor in the desire to resettle.

Before we look closely at the case of Bragg's, Deer and Green's Islands, let me emphasize that all the cases I am familiar with vary enormously in terms of reasons for resettling and post-moving, socio-economic conditions. In the case of our Bonavista Bay islands, the following factors played a role in the people's motives in moving to larger communities:

1. **Isolation**—Ice prevented travel to the mainland during the winter and spring months. The nearest hospital was at Brookfield, 30 miles away by boat even in good weather.

2. **Infrastructure deficiencies**—The islands lacked electricity and phones, which had become commonplace elsewhere in the province. Also, mail service was generally unreliable.

3. **Scope of people's outlook**—Although it is unusual for outport people, those of Bragg's Island and vicinity were highly mobile. They fished off Labrador in the summer and in the winter worked as loggers in the Glovertown area (on the mainland). Therefore, they had some cash income and some familiarity with larger centres, and a relatively developed world view.

4. **Emphasis on education**—This feature, too, was uncommon among outport Newfoundland. But traditionally the island people are well educated and accomplished and many of them occupy leadership positions in Newfoundland society.[8] The straw that broke the camel's back, then, was the inability to get a teacher to live on the island.

5. **The presence of a leader**—In some outports, there emerged someone who led the campaign to resettle. In other cases, the government fulfilled this role. And in a few cases, community leaders urged residents not to resettle. In the Bragg's Island situation, an older established schooner owner began the pressure to leave the community *en masse*. (Incidentally, this man was accused of being unscrupulous in his methods, as were other leaders elsewhere. But it should be noted that he was tried and acquitted.)[9]

After the decision to move, the work had just begun. The people of Sound Island, Placentia Bay, decided to move because they could not get a schoolteacher for their children. The story of how they moved their houses to Garden Cove on the mainland is

---

8 For example, the nine families of Green's Island produced 27 teachers, 19 of whom had Bachelor's degrees.

9 This shows the need for special advisors for those who resettled or wished to.

nothing short of amazing. First of all, the people had to cut wood and build slipways in both Sound Island and Garden Cove. Then they fitted oil drums in the houses so they would float more easily. The work was done in the cold month of February, 1953. Iverson and Matthews put us at the scene:[10]

> ...all the men assembled with ropes and tackles and slowly began to move the first house. But, when the house was on the slipway, all caution had to be abandoned. A house lowered slowly will fill with water and ground. Thus, the houses had to slide quickly down the slipway, no matter how great the danger of breakage. Once in the water, a house will float for about ten minutes before it sinks to the level of the first floor ceiling. In this brief interval the boats had to be attached to the lead rope and the house towed into deep water. Then began the slow, agonizing two mile pull, with the boats strung along the lead rope, and most powerful at the head.

Once in Garden Cove the work became even more excruciating. The men pulled the houses onto land using rollers as bulldozers did not arrive until much later. One hundred and fifty fishermen lined up on the tow rope for 300 yards. They dragged fourteen houses, a few inches at a time, up the hills to their sites. It is astonishing that only one window was broken (the movements of the bulldozer, though, caused a wall to split). As the authors sum it up, "That so much could be done under these conditions with so little loss is a testimony to the pluck and ingenuity of these fishermen."[11] (I should add that the people of Oderin, Placentia Bay, moved a *church* in this way, to Little Bay near Marystown, which is about ten miles by sea.) Sadly, Iverson and Matthews who interviewed the resettled people, concluded that for most of them the move was not worth it; their standard of living and independence had declined dramatically after thirteen years in the still semi-isolated Garden Cove.

---

[10] Iverson and Matthews, p. 35.

[11] Ibid., p. 35.

The following table pertains to the people of Bragg's Island and vicinity ten to twelve years after they resettled. It is interesting in that it illustrates the shift from a largely unmechanized subsistence economy to a more technological cash-based economy.

Table 3
Ownership of Appliances Before and After Moving*

Appliances	Households with appliances before moving	Households which have appliances today (1968)
Telephone	—	19
TV	—	17
Radio	20	16
Record player	2	7
Washer	1	19
Sewing machine	13	14
Vacuum cleaner	—	7
Wood stove	20	9
Oil/electric stove	—	16
Fridge	—	16
Floor polisher	—	9
Deep freeze	—	1
Electric organ	—	3
Furnace	—	4
Car or truck	—	11

*Iverson and Matthews, p. 49.

The researchers conclude that the Bragg's Islanders enjoyed an improvement in their material conditions after they left their former home. The key to their success was the availability of paid employment (mainly for men), an ingredient that was unfortunately absent in the case of the men who painstakingly hauled their houses from Sound Island to Garden Cove.

Resistance to resettlement

Many observers now regard the resettlement programs as a dismal failure. I am inclined to agree, although you may not, because the ad hoc nature of the programs meant that people's former way of life was not replaced with an even more satisfactory way of life. Gradually, this has dawned on the people of rural Newfoundland. There have been three main forms of resistance or protest:

1. Refusal to resettle, as in the case of Fogo Island (assisted by MUN Extension);
2. Returning to live in former communities and reviving them, as summer fishing stations (Red Island in Placentia Bay, for example);.
3. Holding resettlement reunions in the old communities, for weddings (CBC's *Land and Sea* did a program on this) or just for old times' sake (the reunited people of Merasheen even compiled an album of their traditional songs).

As a sociologist, I feel that the negative impact of the resettlement schemes on the Newfoundland psyche cannot be underestimated; in essence, resettlement told people that their culture and way of life was invalid, certainly from a modern perspective. The socio-economic indicators are that economic stability did not result from the attempt at setting up growth centres. There is evidence that GPP has little direct relevance to the geographical pattern of development.[12] One of the lessons we should learn from the resettlement period is that *regional policy* must not be a scaled-down

[12] Moseley, 1974, and others.

version of national policy if it is to be appropriate and therefore more likely to be effective. We will focus on the concept of regional policy in a later lecture in this section. For now let's turn to what I have already referred to as the government dependency phase (the second distinctive phase in industrial development in post-Confederation Newfoundland).

Sociological term

Regional policy—social policy with a spatial or geographic dimension; policy that is designed for a particular region rather than the country as a whole.

Lecture 3

Government dependency and regional policy

The government dependency phase

The dream of an industrialized Newfoundland died a slow and painful death. Many of the mega-projects created large-scale employment only for short periods of time; subsequently, spinoff effects were not long-lasting.[13] In addition, there were never enough of these projects and they were never permanent enough to transform Newfoundland into a New England or Southern Ontario. There was never any significant effort to build up small-scale, rural-based projects, and the all-important fishing industry was virtually ignored as it did not fit into governments' plans.

During the construction boom and mega-project era, Newfoundland became transformed into a cash economy. More and more, as the "baby bonus" and paycheques came into homes, traditional economic adaptations were forgotten, including kitchen gardens and hunting, for example. Rural Newfoundlanders became for the first time ever *consumers*, buying household items with cash instead of producing such items themselves. The age-old egalitarian ethic on the island was undoubtedly negatively affected by the introduction of this sort of materialism. We may have felt richer but we were just as

[13] This may turn out to be true of the Hibernia mega-project, as well.

vulnerable to downturns in the economy as we had been to the unpredictabilities of nature.

This vulnerability became poignantly evident when the paying jobs dried up, and people now used to receiving wages were forced onto the unemployment insurance rolls. They now had needs that required cash: fuel for skidoos and boats; clothing for children for the school year; and household durables that Newfoundlanders, like other North Americans, now took for granted. Yet there were not enough jobs available to satisfy everyone's material needs. In most outports there were only one or two employment possibilities (e.g., the fish plant, town office, etc.) and very often these were seasonal. In a report commissioned for the Community Services Council, MUN sociologist Robert Hill found that, in 1980, 41.6% of the unemployed in Newfoundland had only one potential employer; a further 33.2% had between two and six possible employers.[14] Hence, three quarters of the province's unemployed had less than seven potential employers. This weak labour market means the concept of 'job search' is all but irrelevant in the Newfoundland setting. It is logical that in the absence of other money-earning prospects, the population became heavily dependent upon government assistance, particularly U.I., which in Newfoundland does not carry the stigma that social assistance payments do.

Earlier I said that there is a strong tradition in both Canada and Newfoundland of government activity in the economy. In the early 1970s, the provincial government instituted a Department of Rural Development to provide support for the burgeoning rural development associations in Newfoundland. The federal government made its development efforts through a succession of departments, beginning with DREE (the Department of Regional Economic Expansion) in 1969. DREE programs, however, continued to be influenced by GPP, instead of being tailor-made for Newfoundland and other economically peripheral regions in Canada. Accordingly DREE's (and its successor's) programs have tended to be urban in orientation and so they have concentrated their activities in cities like St. John's.

In the second phase of development in post-Confederation Newfoundland, government had a different sort of presence in our

---

[14] Hill, 1983.

rural communities. One job creation scheme followed another, including: Local Initiatives Program; Young Canada Works; Canada Works; and a host of other make-work programs. For many years these projects have been one of the few sources of employment in some outports and towns. In combination with U.I., they have enable people to make a living. According to the Royal Commission on Employment and Unemployment:[15]

> During the 1970s, and even more so during the 1980s, make-work projects and the 'ten week syndrome' have become part of outport life. For the people involved this is simply one more in a long line of rational economic adaptations to the few economic opportunities available to them.

Newfoundlanders now have the same material expectations as other North Americans but we do not have the economic infrastructure or wherewithal to satisfy these expectations. As the Royal Commission clearly demonstrated, self-reliance, once a highly-regarded value on this island, has been lost or at least badly eroded.

Regional policy

The socio-economic indicators in present-day Newfoundland tell us that the two forms of development initiatives outlined above were generally not effective in spurring successful economic activity and growth in Newfoundland. Economists and sociologists offer a plethora of reasons why this is so. A crucial part of beginning to answer the question 'why' is attempting to understand the meaning of *regional policy* (which many social scientists believe is necessary for development). Regional policy consists largely of stabilization measures aimed at a certain region; it is policy with a spatial or location dimension.[16] It should also have a cultural dimension; that is, it should also take into account the culture of the people it was

[15] *Building on Our Strengths*, 1986, p. 50.

[16] Richardson, 1969.

intended for. The aim of regional policy should be to achieve "as much economic and social equality as possible without undermining current cultural and social structures."[17] To be successful, regional policy cannot be "a miniature version of national economic planning."[18] The unemployment insurance scheme for fishermen is an example of how regulations that are inappropriate can undermine traditional social structures. (The student is referred to a 1988 policy paper I wrote called "Living on the Dead," which is in the course book of readings.) Within this frame of reference we can see that the above policy initiatives for Newfoundland would not likely succeed in their objectives. The dream of an industrial Newfoundland and the patchwork quilt of government dependency were poor substitutes for the regional policy that Newfoundland so badly needed.

Sociological term

Consumer—participants in the capitalist economy, using money to purchase goods rather than produce them oneself.

---

[17] Matthews, 1983, p. 220.

[18] Richardson, 1969, p. 116.

Lecture 4

Life as an industrial worker

There are many moving accounts of the difficulties and even tragedies suffered by industrial workers. Here in Newfoundland, many of them relate to the sea. There is the horrifying example of the "Ocean Ranger" oil rig that went down with all lives lost in a February storm in 1983. There are also the sealing disasters mentioned in another chapter in this section and countless fishing mishaps, in which it is usually family members who are involved. We know then, from folksongs, literature and life experience, that industrial accidents, often involving loss of life, are an integral part of the history of work and employment in our society. Marxist analysts would see this as the logical outcome of capitalist business practices; labour is expendable as part of the cost of doing business. Workers are exploited because there are so many of them, they can be easily replaced—certainly in the Newfoundland case. The pursuit of profit, Marxists say, is so important to capitalists or business people that occupational health and safety is neglected as it isn't related to profit-making. As part of the same theme, they argue that workers are forced to take risks because of economic oppression. Loggers, for example, take insufficient precautions while cutting trees because they have to rush to fill quotas. Of course, many non-Marxists would agree with this or a similar analysis. Your job as a student of Newfoundland society and culture is to analyze the problem yourself. Ideally, it would be studied *cross-culturally* to see if our industrial problems are moderate or severe compared to those in similar areas.

It is clear, for our purposes, that there are significant numbers of Newfoundlanders getting injured on the job. In 1990, the number requiring medical assistance of some sort was 19,206; 10,404 (or 54%) of these workers submitted successful claims for monetary compensation. In addition to this, the Department of Labour (Newfoundland government) reports that 24 Newfoundland workers died on the job during 1990. Undoubtedly, many of you know of cases of individuals who were killed at work: on construction sites, while fishing, in manufacturing plants, during hunting trips or elsewhere on the job. In many cases the deceased workers were able to leave their families with insurance funds or compensation, but this is by no means universal in Newfoundland. In the past such cases would have been the exception by far with most families of dead fishermen, sealers and miners receiving absolutely no cash.

Health and safety on the schooners

For a cursory look at working conditions and health and safety in the fishing industry historically we can look to the research of MUN Anthropologist Raoul Andersen. In the 1980s Andersen examined records on injury, illness and death among American schooners and dory banks fishermen between 1852 and 1912.[19] We know that sea disasters occurred not infrequently and that they very often claimed the lives of the ship's entire crew. This is immortalized in many of our folksongs, such as "Cape St. Mary's" and "The Loss of the Marion." However, Andersen wanted to know more about the day-to-day health and injury experience of 19th and 20th century fishermen.

Andersen concentrated on 64 cases in the 1890s, most of which occurred during the east coast fishing season, June through August. At the time there were 60 doctors in Newfoundland, with one quarter of these practicing in St. John's. Most of these doctors had been trained in Britain, Ireland, Scotland and the U.S. According to information gleaned from U.S. Consul records, the offshore illnesses, injuries and deaths break down as follows:

---

[19] These crews consisted of Americans, immigrants and many Newfoundlanders and Nova Scotians. The men concerned were all brought to Newfoundland ports.

Table 4
Illness and injury of fishermen in the 19th and 20th centuries

Infectious disorder		Injuries		Other	
LaGrippe (influenza)	7	Badly bruised	1	Diabetes	1
Quinsey	1	Broken leg	2	Bright's disease	1
Quinsey & rupture	1	Broken knee cap	1	Dropsy	1
Consumption (TB)	2	Sprained limbs	1	Rheumatism	1
Diphtheria	3	Hand injuries	3	Sudden death	1
Fever	1	Blood poisoning	1	Unspecified, illness	19
Pleurisy	1	Unspecified	7	Unspecified	8
Total	16	Total	16	Total	32

Source : "Nineteenth Century American Banks Fishing Under Sail: Its Health and Injury Costs," Raoul Andersen, *Canadian Folklore*, Vol. 12, 2, 1990, p. 104.

(Before we discuss these data, it's important to note that, as with the majority of research projects, Andersen encountered some methodology problems. For example, it is not known how many American vessels and fishermen operated in Newfoundland waters each year. In addition, illnesses, injuries and sometimes deaths were often unrecorded. We must bear these limitations in mind while analyzing these, and other, statistics.)

As the author points out, many of the recorded illnesses were no surprise (e.g., fever, infections, consumption and others) considering the time and working conditions, as well as the state of medical science in that period. On the other hand, Andersen expresses surprise that 'nervous exhaustion' was not mentioned (it is reported elsewhere), in spite of the heavy work and long hours. Similarly, alcoholism, also mentioned, was likely a problem as binge-drinking was known to be common while the ships were in port. Finally, scurvy, beri-beri and smallpox would most likely have occurred frequently due to poor hygiene practices and facilities, limited fresh water and overcrowded sleeping and eating areas. One possibility for these oversights, if that is what they are, is that diagnosis was difficult. Also, conditions on the American schooners were superior to those of the Newfoundland schooners. It's probable the illnesses above were seen more frequently on Newfoundland vessels. To back up this contention, Andersen quotes Newfoundland Captain Arch Thornhill:[20]

> There was more on their tables than a few leftover beans, like I have seen myself many times. It wasn't until the mid-1930s that we ever got a case of milk for our schooners. We had molasses, but milk, sugar, tinned fruit, fresh meat and such foods were called 'extras' by our owners. And the crews had to pay for *all* of it.

Injuries included: broken and blown off hands; blindness and other gunpowder injuries; blood poisoning from fish hooks; and hernia due to hard physical labour, in particular hauling and pulling heavy nets. Death was less common but had far-reaching social implications. In the 1890s and early 20th century, widows received a one-time government grant of $80.00 from the "Bank Fishermen's Insurance Fund."[21] There were also relief charities and possibilities of extended family support but impoverished widows and their

---

[20] Andersen, p. 111.

[21] Each year, a fisherman (or the merchant who supplied him) would contribute fifty cents to the Insurance Fund.

children were a significant part of the fish flake work force in outport Newfoundland, as they struggled to survive on their own. Other schooner widows, like my grandmother who lost her husband in the Burin Peninsula August Gale of 1935, moved to St. John's to enter domestic service and the foreign urban economy. Many of these women were forced to put their children in orphanages due to their inability to make ends meet. Life as a fisherman's wife was a stressful one but life as a fisherman's widow was even more tenuous. Meanwhile, the lives of the men at sea were anything but easy.

Health and safety in the St. Lawrence mines

Another relevant case study that we will use to illustrate these problems is the case of the fluorspar mines in Lawn, St. Lawrence and other communities on "the boot" of the Burin Peninsula. For this discussion I will rely on a saddening book by anthropologist Elliott Leyton entitled *Dying Hard: the Ravages of Industrial Carnage*. The work consists of ten in-depth, open-ended interviews with miners and their spouses/widows and it is not a pleasure to read. When Leyton carried out his study in the early 1970s, one household in every three had a dead or dying miner (St. Lawrence and Lawn). No family was untouched by what Leyton calls "industrial carnage" and many families were subjected to a multitude of tragedies. Almost every man who worked in the mines before 1960 (when Alcan took over and installed ventilation) is dead.

The mine, discovered by New Yorker Walter Siebert, opened in 1937 when medical science had knowledge of silicosis.[22] Legislation pertaining to this disease had been passed in societies as repressive as South Africa in as early as 1911. But for the miners of St. Lawrence there was no protection from the deadly dust; there were no

[22] The two most fatal diseases contracted by miners were silicosis and lung cancer. The silicosis did not come from the fluorspar itself but from dry drilling in the host granite in unventilated spaces. The lung cancer originated from an immense low-grade uranium deposit near the mine.

regulations governing the operations of the mining firm until 1951. We have to look at the socio-economic conditions of the time to see why men from all over the area wanted so badly to become miners. Leyton points to the precarious economy of the peninsula which had been disturbed by a number of disasters (tidal waves, the collapse of international trade ["the Crash"] in 1929) just before the mines went into operation. Although it *may* be somewhat exaggerated, Leyton offers a Royal Commission quote that provides some explanation:[23]

> ...many witnesses have testified that in those depression days a half-starved man was considered fortunate to hold a job where he could spend ten hours or so each day, drenched in the waters of Black Duck and half choked with dust from his hammer, trying to earn enough money to keep his family from starving, in an environment where fuel was just as scarce as food.

Prior to the opening of the St. Lawrence mines, the southern half of the Burin Peninsula had consisted of a fishing society that operated along the same lines as the hundreds of other such communities in Newfoundland (this is documented elsewhere in this book). Not surprisingly, this changed as the men marched off to the mines. The problems were exacerbated as sickness invaded the towns, according to Leyton. We may put these changes into five categories:

1. **Social Stratification.** A once egalitarian fishing society became class conscious as workers were graded by rank and salary. People were no longer judged merely by how hard they worked and social privilege was extended to company rank.
2. **Identity Construction.** Related to this is the fact that individuals, as well as communities as a whole, constructed their identities around the mining industry rather than traditional fishing culture.
3. **Social Conflict.** This was perhaps a natural outgrowth of the

[23] Leyton, p. 14.

complication of social stratification in St. Lawrence and Lawn. It manifested itself in the snubbing of low-ranking workers by management and their wives, for example. Social conflict was intensified by the seemingly arbitrary manner in which compensation and welfare payments were dispersed.

4. **Economic Hardship.** Certainly, this was not unknown in Newfoundland but it must have been particularly hard to adjust to for people who had become accustomed to regular wage incomes. Many miners' families became poor after husbands became disabled or died; economic opportunities for these widows were severely limited in rural Newfoundland at that time (and remain so). Many people felt they did not receive enough compensation; and those who had no compensation struggled to get by on monthly welfare payments.

5. **Changes in Family Structure**. Demographically, the picture of families in the St. Lawrence-Lawn area during the 1960s and 70s would have been different from elsewhere in Newfoundland, due to the absence of fathers/husbands. The women in these communities were forced to adjust and expand their roles in the family system.

Following this lecture is an excerpt from Dr. Leyton's book from an interview with Victoria Janes, whose husband died of lung cancer contracted in the mines. Victoria's husband was one of about two hundred who became diseased and died because of the mines. Although Victoria's story took place in Newfoundland, it's important to note that her experience of the hardships of widowhood are universal and that each year hundreds of thousands of industrial deaths occur worldwide. By bringing this issue down to the micro level, as we do with Victoria's story, we are able to see the day-to-day human side of industrial carnage.

Reading

(excerpts from)

Chapter 10: They didn't do their duty

by Elliott Leyton

And then it was September '64 that Dr. Hollywood sent him into St. John's...Well, we never had very much money because at that time for the Sick Benefit you were only getting thirty dollars a week. But my father and father-in-law were very good to me, so I went in.

My God! Oh, he was terrible. He was very upset. He had letters there and they weren't opened, and cards. It wasn't him. I didn't know how to go about it... I didn't go in anymore then until October. He was bright and he wanted to come home. He was very sick looking and had lost a tremendous amount of weight, down to about 135 pounds from 190.

I always tried to keep the conversation interesting. Tell him about the children and what they were doing. The second time I

From *Dying Hard: The Ravages of Industrial Carnage* by Elliott Leyton, 1975, pp. 115, 116, 117 and 119. Used by permission of the Canadian Publishers, McClelland and Stewart Limited, Toronto, Ontario.
These excerpts are as told to Elliott Leyton by Victoria Janes (fictitious name); wife of Jim Janes, the subject of the piece.

went in, he didn't ask me about the children or anything, and that made me believe there was something radically wrong. So then I went to see Dr. Farrell: he told me what it was, Lung Cancer. That's confirmed now; I mean I knew deep in my heart what it was, right?...

...The first few days he came home, he made two trips. One down to the meadow and he looked all around the harbour. Then he went down there. And that was the last time he was out through the door. He'd get up; he'd try to get up and he'd come out and have something to eat.

And then he got that he couldn't walk. He found it very difficult to walk. I couldn't handle him. It was very difficult for me to try to bring him around; besides, I had six children here. I didn't know how to handle a sick person. I mean some people are fit; his brother could come over, poor Jim was in bed, put his hand under him and handle him. He had this training, St. John Ambulance; but I couldn't, I only knew the one way to drag him. And he wasn't eating. So Dr. Hollywood come to a decision, and he asked Jim would he like to come in with him for a while, in the hospital. He said, "Yes, I would. I'd like to come in 'cause maybe you'd do something for me." So we brought him in. We brought him to the hospital on a stretcher the 22nd day of December, 1964. I went to the hospital every day, every afternoon, every after supper. I missed one night, and that night you couldn't get through the door, too stormy. But afternoon and night. Someone would come with me, my sister-in-law or his sister or someone. He'd always have somebody. He died February the 15th. But now I would say for a month or six weeks before he died, sometimes he'd sing out to a crowd he worked with. You know, he'd be saying, "Pull up the line, boy; go down and get the pump." He was living things that he used to do, working...

...After Jim died[24]...I was really lonely. I used to expect these people to come when a certain time come in the night. That was hard to adjust to, too. You'd be waiting for the people to come, or you'd be waiting for him to knock to say he wanted something or to do something with the children. But of course, after a while I got used to that too.

---

24 Added by Dr. Hanrahan for clarity.

...I always put my children first. I hope they turn out to make something of themselves, because I always put them first and I always put myself last. I think that's the answer. There was nothing easy about it, but when I look back I don't regret anything that I've done. I think everything was done that could be done.

Sociological term

Cross-cultural—cross-cultural studies were first developed by anthropologists. These studies compare one culture to another with a view to establishing which features are unique and which are common to the human condition itself.

Lecture 5

The fishing industry

Introduction

There is one *institution* more than any other that Newfoundlanders and non-Newfoundlanders alike associate with this province...that is, of course, the fishing industry. The fishery is, according to popular and traditional culture, almost synonymous with life in Newfoundland, especially rural Newfoundland. The fishery ties us together: people fish for cod on the Northern Peninsula and they fish for cod on the Burin Peninsula. Men and women process fish in Marystown and they do so in St. Anthony. Although we may be hundreds of miles from each other, participation in and reliance on the fishery contribute to our sharing a similar world-view, or *culture*. This is not to say that those of us who don't take part in the fishery are not true Newfoundlanders (although I have heard people make that often hurtful mistake); surely, the people of Grand Falls, Gander and Buchans have as much of a Newfoundland identity as the rest of us.

The importance of the fishery in our culture comes largely from its central role in *defining* Newfoundland society and culture. You will remember that the fishery was this island's *raison d'être*, as far as European settlement was concerned. Our ancestors defied government orders so that they could fish here. For centuries, Britain, France and other countries fought intensely over the fish off our shores. Historically, the fishery has been the largest industry, in terms of employment, in Newfoundland. Even today its presence is everywhere. To give you an example, from July 9, 1991 when I lived in the Water Street East area of St. John's, I saw trap skiffs heading out to the fishing grounds; I heard reports on the fishery on two radio stations; I wondered if the caplin will ever come in this year; I worried about the economic cost of having the fishery fail because of the late ice; at MUN today, I taught a large number of fishermen's sons and daughters; I noticed representations and symbols of the industry (i.e., ornamental schooners) around the university; and I am today, as always, the granddaughter of fishermen. It's only 2:00 p.m. and I haven't even seen any television news yet. I suspect that the fishing industry is this pervasive in most of your lives as well.

People in and outside of this province are aware of how we recognize and even honour the fishery and those who work in it in traditional Newfoundland folksongs. Some examples of these are: "Let Me Fish Off Cape St. Mary's", "Jack was Every Inch a Sailor", "The Squid Jigging Ground", and even the once extremely popular "Rubber Boots Song" is about a fisherman and his lover. It is certainly fair to say that the fisherman is prominent in much of what we may consider traditional Newfoundland folklore. And did you ever notice how many paintings and photographs of fishing boats and harbours artists produce, no matter if they have fishery connections or not? This is especially true if they are trying to capture the soul or essence of Newfoundland: I think Gerry Squires' Stations of the Cross set in a fishing setting are good examples of this. (These were commissioned for a Mount Pearl Church.) For example, Christ is nailed to the cross on a rugged, rocky Newfoundland beach.

While all of this is true, our view of fishermen and women and their industry is dual in a sense; that is, there is an equal and increasing body of thought inside and out of this province that views fishermen as backward, always happy-go-lucky and not-too-bright. Newfie jokes are perhaps the most vivid and well-publicized example of this. Some of the Newfoundland souvenirs are also patronizing caricatures of people who fish and, as a colleague of mine pointed out several years ago, a number of local theatre productions have portrayed the fisherman, our cultural symbol, as ignorant and crude.

Perhaps some knowledge of social psychology is required to interpret the origins and meaning of this dichotomy. At first glance it is as if some insidious self-loathing has seeped into the Newfoundland culture, possibly as a result of the urban-industrial phase we went through and the resettlement that was a part of it. I feel that many of us have bought into the popular North American mythology that our lifestyles are inferior to those of people in urban areas like New York and Toronto. (I feel certain, by the way, that this will turn around as environmental problems in cities increase.) There are others, of course, who profit commercially through the exploitation of a large and central population group in our society and it is not in their interest to reform this particular outlook. Hence, social change is not likely to come from these quarters. You no doubt are aware by now that I think there are other ways to be funny or entertain without *stereotyping* and denigrating particular social or occupational groups. I think Newfie jokes and the like erode our collective self-esteem (and that is something we certainly don't need). This is one area where sociological study and analysis would be beneficial.

I have heard it said that it is almost impossible to overstate the importance of the fishing industry to Newfoundland. As I've said at the beginning of this lecture, the fishery has been significant to us for cultural reasons; it is a central part of the Newfoundland identity, both as we perceive it and as outsiders perceive it. In addition, there are economic reasons; this industry employs tens of thousands of workers, year-round and seasonal, in its harvesting and processing sectors. The *economic spinoff* from this kind of employment generation is undoubtedly enormous; think of the gear, supplies and household items a fisherman or woman will buy in the course of a year. It's also necessary to remember that, as an export-oriented industry, the fishery brings in *new* money to our economy; we receive American dollars, for example, in exchange for our fish products. It is only fishermen and other *primary producers* (i.e., farmers) who *create* income for the province in this way; the rest of us who are employed are merely involved in the recirculation of money, rather than its creation.

Besides its prominence in Newfoundland society and economy, another characteristic of this industry is its heterogenous nature. In other words, there is a variety of sectors in the industry (e.g., the offshore, midshore and inshore), a multitude of species harvested (e.g., cod, mackerel, shellfish), many levels of technology used (i.e., basic versus advanced), and a stratification of skills and of incomes. There is also a great deal of regional variation with regard to all of these factors. An inshore dragger skipper in Anchor Point will live a very different life from a small boat fisherman in Aquaforte, south of St. John's. (By the way this is the kind of thing that makes this industry so fascinating for a sociologist.) In spite of these differences, though, fishermen and women across the island have a great deal in common with one another: concerns about cod stocks, for example, and problems dealing with the licensing and unemployment insurance systems.

Unionization in the Newfoundland fishery

Since the fishery is so multi-faceted, I've decided to focus on one particular aspect of the industry, unionization. Much of the material I used is from *More Than Just a Union: the Story of the NFFAWU* by Gordon Inglis, an anthropologist. I am also drawing on material from my M.A. and Ph.D. theses and from Peter Sinclair's book, *From Traps to Draggers.*

The credit system

Before we look at the rise of unions representing fishermen and women in Newfoundland, some background information is required. According to Peter Sinclair, the fisherman's primary problem was his (or her) dependence on the merchant for all information and contact with the outside world. We might conceptualize the relationship this way:

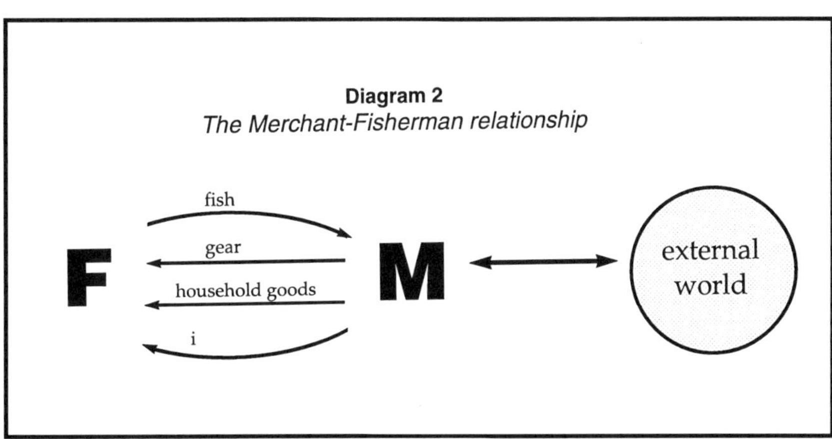

In most cases, the fisherman had no choice but to sell fish to one particular merchant; most outport merchants enjoyed a monopoly situation:[25]

> Thus the local merchant was the point of mediation or linkage between *domestic commodity producers* and the wider capitalist economy. As a supplier of small quantities of cod to the international market-place, the individual merchant was in no position to control the selling price, but he could ascertain the movement of the market and was in a position to ensure a return on his transactions with fishermen by altering the price paid for cod and/or by manipulating the grading system. For example, fish sold to Europe as a top quality product might be down-graded at the point of purchase from fishermen.

The fisherman and the merchant were partners in an unequal power relationship. The merchant, although not all-powerful and occasionally subject to economic troubles, had more control over his (or her) economic situation than did the fishermen. Under the *truck system*, as it was called, the merchant enjoyed far more political power, social influence, prestige and wealth than the vast majority of fishermen. Fishermen rarely managed to accumulate any surplus; normally, the fisherman and his family began the fishing season in debt to the merchant and finished the season with a small profit, if any. This, of course, made it almost impossible for fishermen to better their economic status, as savings were needed to do this. In this way the system perpetuated itself, as seen in the following diagram:

---

[25] Sinclair, 1985, pp. 45–46.

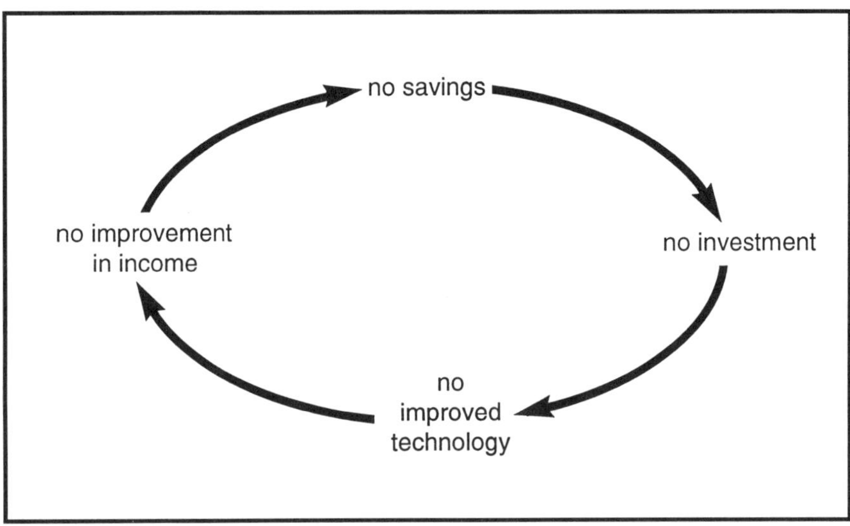

In *From Traps to Draggers,* Sinclair describes actual cases from the end of the fishing season of 1949 on the Great Northern Peninsula (see the table below). If this situation is representative, then it is clear that the truck system favoured the merchant class as we have discussed earlier. (While this is the way the system worked, I would like to emphasize that both the fishing classes and the merchant classes were heterogenous. It's important to remember this so we will not oversimplify their relationship.) Let's look at the industry of more recent times.

Table 5: 1949 Merchants' Accounts

Merchant Accounts Examined*	Number	Percentage
Balance owing to fishermen	45	9%
Balance owing to merchant	98	20%
Nothing owed	343	71%
Total	486	100%

*Adapted from the text of Sinclair, 1985, p. 46.

The NFFAWU and Newfoundland's trawlermen

This lecture does not attempt to recant the entire history of unionization in the fishing industry; its primary goal is to detail the social and economic conditions of life in rural Newfoundland for thousands of fishing families in various eras. Let's look at a more modern period now, and at a union many of you are no doubt familiar with.

Several decades after Coaker and the F.P.U. had been active, the Newfoundland Fish, Food and Allied Workers' Union (or "The Fishermen's Union") was launched at a St. John's Convention in April, 1971. Anthropologist David Macdonald reports in his book that the emerging union was coolly received by employers, although in most cases, employers took little action to prevent it from taking hold. The government of the day, under Smallwood, was not, he says, actively opposed to union organization in the fishery either. Originally the NFFAWU was a coming together of the Canadian Food and Allied Workers' Union (CFAW) and the Northern Fishermen's Union (NFU) which had been formed in 1969 in Port au Choix. The NFU's first objectives were remarkably similar to those of the long-defunct F.P.U.:[26]

> To promote the economic interests of fishermen; to work with and promote other organizations and causes working for the betterment of the fishermen; to develop...a comprehensive fishery development plan for the region; to make agreements for the purchasing of fuel, gear and other goods on a collective basis.

The truck system had vanished by this time as Newfoundland's became increasingly a cash economy following Confederation. However, fishermen and those who supported unionization

[26] Macdonald, 1985, pp. 49–50.

felt that the structure of the fishing industry continued to let most of the power and wealth accumulate and remain in the hands of the fish merchants. By the early 1970s the offshore trawler fishery was dominated by five large firms, largely family-owned and some linked through partnership connections. The largest of "the Big Five," as they were known, was Fishery Products Limited.[27] Together these companies employed almost 9000 fish plant workers and deep-sea fishermen; in addition, they were the main and often only buyer for thousands of inshore fishermen.

The trawler or industrial, offshore-based firms were integrated. This meant that company owners and managers set the prices for transferring the fish from the boats to the fish plants. With fishermen having no say, prices were kept artificially low; in fact, the trawler sector normally operated at a loss. This was done, according to economist Parcival Copes, so firms would have to pay no income tax and then could qualify for financial assistance from government. (And low fish prices also kept fishermen's earnings depressed.) The "loss" was then made up in the processing sector. This accounting system benefited the plant owners but obviously not the fishermen. It was this system and the working conditions of fishermen that laid the foundation for the formation of a union.

While the vessels used by the Big Five were part of 20th century technology, certain features of the offshore trawler fishery smack of a pre-industrial era. This is perhaps best illustrated through an examination of the illegal trawlermen's strike of 1974. These fishermen would often be on deck in dangerous weather for sixty hours at a stretch. The only regular break would come at meal times and the crew would stay in quarters that were usually dirty and cramped. There were no mattresses or blankets provided by the company. It is even more startling that there was no compensation for injuries in an industry with injury and death rates higher than for almost any other industrial occupation.

The system of payment for trawlermen was also unfair. Up until the dispute in question, trawlermen were considered to be "co-venturers"; accordingly they were not paid a salary and instead

---

[27] The others were Nickersons (based in Nova Scotia), T.J. Hardy, National Sea Products and the Lake Group.

got paid on the basis of a share of the catch. The crew's share was 37% (between approximately 13 workers) and money was deducted from each pay packet to help cover the cost of provisions.[28] "Learners" were paid slightly less and officers and cooks, more. Consistent with the traditional *patron-client* relationship, captains made their own arrangements with the company. Besides outfitting themselves, trawler fishermen were obligated to pay a portion of the fuel and ice costs of the trip. After a trip with a low catch, trawlermen could and sometimes did end up owing the company money.[29] Working conditions did not match those of most industrial workers at the time. The average trawler voyage would last ten days and have a turnaround time of forty-eight hours. A trawlerman's annual holiday consisted of one week at Christmas and two or three weeks off when the vessel was in refit. On board, the men worked long, gruelling hours, often in horrific weather conditions. Onshore, their wives carried all the burdens of running a household and raising a family, virtually alone.

By the early 1970s a fishermen's union had been formed in Newfoundland as we have seen, and shortly afterwards, conditions in the offshore harvesting sector were ripe for strike action. Supported by their union, trawlermen were fed up with their system of pay and the conditions they worked under. In 1974, they walked off the trawlers in an illegal strike, feeling more confident than not that a settlement in their favour would result...eventually. An early blow to the strikers occurred when the provincial government refused to get involved, despite the union's requests that it do so. The Newfoundland Fisheries Minister, John Crosbie, displayed a remarkable indifference to the entire process by going on a foreign holiday during the strike.

Finally, as public pressure mounted, the province did get involved by commissioning a report on the offshore sector by Dr. Leslie Harris, a historian at Memorial. While not all of Dr. Harris' recommended changes were implemented, the changes that were made were of a fundamental nature. The most significant of these is

---

[28] The offshore seal hunt operated on much the same basis for most of its history, as we shall see in a later lecture.

[29] Again, this is similar to the offshore seal hunt.

the end of the co-venturer system which had been inherently unjust in that it benefited the powerful fish companies at the expense of the workers. In 1974 it was agreed that trawlermen would be paid $20 per day[30] in addition to a fixed rate for every pound of fish harvested. Under the new system, trawlermen would earn 80% to 90% more on low catch trips than they had in the past. In the case of a more successful harvest, trawlermen would be paid approximately 50% more. They were also to receive benefits like 4% vacation pay, a company-funded life insurance plan, and provisions like mattresses.

Not surprisingly, resentment toward the fish firms was widespread at the time of the trawlermen's strike. Perhaps for the first time, Newfoundlanders began to view the large-scale, industrial harvesting sector as an unjust and exploitive arena. This resentment was expressed eloquently in one of the leading newspapers of the time: "Who but the merchants, steeped in historical arrogance, would dare cling to the idea of equal risk, more or less, between a trawlerman and his co-venturer fish baron?"[31]

With the end of the co-venturer system, the socio-economic status of most trawlermen rose significantly. On the Burin Peninsula, the site of several trawler ports, work on a trawler became coveted, if increasingly scarce. In many communities, the families of trawlermen became the economic elite with steady, guaranteed salaries of $20,000, $30,000 and more as the years went by. Compared to the inshore fishery with its uncertainties, offshore fishermen were doing well. However, it is worth mentioning that there is still room for improvement in the offshore sector: trawlermen still spend long hours on deck in dangerous weather conditions, and lengths of voyages, turnaround times and holidays have not changed. Except for greater economic security (and lately even that is far from guaranteed), life for trawlermen's wives and families remains essentially the same. This process of change in the offshore harvesting sector has important implications for class development and class conflict. For example, there is much resentment still

[30] This was the first time they had ever received a salary.

[31] *Daily News*, January 13, 1974, p. 8, cited in Inglis, 1985, p. 226.

toward the co-venturer system and there is increasing hostility between trawlermen and inshore fishermen who claim offshore harvesting has seriously threatened their industry. This may also be an example of how technological and apparent social advances may hurt society and the environment in the long term. Meanwhile, it is my observation that trawlermen constitute the heart of unionization in this province, perhaps largely because of the results of the 1974 strike. In the offshore fishery much has changed while much has remained the same. In the case of the sealing industry, which we will turn to next, the changes have been massive.

Lecture 6

Newfoundland culture and the sealing industry

When I was a teenager in St. John's, I went to the Blessing of the (Seal) Fleet every year. This was an inter-denominational religious ceremony that took place in front of thousands of people; its purpose was to bestow God's favour on the large sealing vessels and their crews as they headed out to "the ice" to harvest seals. I was very impressed with the crowds, the excitement, the nationalism, the ponies and the sight of heroes like Captain Morrissey Johnson and the crew of the Lady Johnson II. I remember feeling so proud to be a Newfoundlander and so integrated into the community. It was as if nationalism and unity permeated the cold March air.

One year a protester who I believe was from Greenpeace chained herself to Captain Johnson's ships. The skipper's reaction was to hack the chain in two and rather violently throw the protester down the gangplank into the emotional crowd. People cheered the captain's actions. They ignored the rantings of Ray Elliott, sealer turned protester, who stood on the back of a pickup truck. There was no violence that I know of. Greenpeace representatives were free to wander unharmed through the thousands gathered on Harbour Drive. I remember staring at them, thinking they were "hippie types" and "out to get us": this view seemed to be unanimous among my peers.

It's my inkling that my experiences related to the seal hunt of the time was typical of those of Newfoundlanders and not just my social group. Sentiments similar to mine were echoed on open line shows and in the province's newspapers. It seemed that everyone was pro-sealing; in fact, to say you weren't was tantamount to betraying Newfoundland.

It's clear that, at least in the milieu I operated in, people felt proud of, defensive about and protective toward the seal hunt. Our task as social scientists is to explain why this is so. My own perception is that economics was only one, even a small, part of our feelings toward the hunt. In the late 1880s, the seal hunt had contributed one-third of Newfoundland's gross national product. Seal products, particularly seal oil, were second only to codfish in terms of economic importance. By the late 1970s, however, sealing was nowhere as significant as it used to be. Around that time approximately 155 people and six vessels went to "the front" each year; this represents a shadow of the old offshore hunt. In addition, there are several studies that show that economic returns to the longliner fleet were inadequate. Later in this lecture I will address the issue of the economic spinoffs of sealing but it's clear that sealing had been declining in economic importance for quite some time. Certainly for the thousands of St. John's residents sealing had no economic value; for others, there would have been some awareness of economics but other factors contributed more to the high level of emotions that developed. Crucial to the question, then, is a consideration of the social and cultural importance of sealing. Let's look at the development of the industry in Newfoundland before returning to this particular issue.

History of sealing

Until the offshore seal hunt was eliminated in 1983, it consisted of vessels steaming out of St. John's but with crews made up of people from both urban and rural Newfoundland. Traditionally, sealers have been mainly from communities along the northeast coast, especially from Bonavista North to Baie Verte and along the Great Northern Peninsula. The seal fishery itself was a major reason for settlement on this part of the island. As Peter Sinclair et al. point out in their study prepared for the Royal Commission on Seals and the Sealing Industry in Canada, the settlement patterns were adapted to exploiting both the inshore and seal fisheries. Communities were small and dispersed, often located on peninsula headlands and offshore islands.

We know from archaeological work by Dr. Jim Tuck and others that the Maritime Archaic Indians utilized the seal resources. Later, John Cabot and Jacques Cartier both took note of the large seal herds off the island. During the late 16th and early 17th centuries, Basque whalers harvested seals for subsistence purposes and possibly to market them with the whales they caught. About one hundred years later the French and English settlers began commercial sealing. Towns like Fogo, Greenspond, Bonavista and Trinity had become major centres for seal oil processing by 1770. Later products like meat and skins become important subsistence items. I think it's both interesting and important to note that sealing played similar roles in other peripheral regions of Canada, such as the Magdalen Islands and Prince Edward Island.

Sealing and economics

Earlier I said that sealing was important because of its impact (or spinoff effect) on Newfoundland communities, as well as because of its contribution to exploit earnings. MUN historian Shannon Ryan found that in 1827 there were 290 ships and 5418 sealers, and that by 1857 these figures had peaked at 370 ships and 13,600 sealers. These numbers were very high considering the fact that Newfoundland's population was perhaps a third of what it is now. Besides this, the seal hunt created jobs in the shipbuilding industry and in pelt and oil processing. Sealing was a critical part of the seasonal round of economic activities in Newfoundland; in fact, its role was central as the development of the spring seal hunt provided a continuous supply of employment during the winter. Sinclair et al. quote L.G. Chafe from *Chafe's Sealing Book* (1923):[32]

> (Formerly,) the winter was a season of carnival, dancing, drinking and playing cards from house to house

[32] Sinclair, 1989, p. 11.

> for those who had money to spend, and a season of wretchedness and destitution for those who had done poorly at the fishery.

There isn't room here to provide a more complete overview of the history and economics of the Newfoundland seal fishery but, as with all the topics I cover in these lectures, if you are interested in learning more, refer to books listed at the end of this lecture. The issue of technological change in the sealing industry is a subject worth exploring, for example.

One of the things I would like to make you aware of concerns the lives of sealers themselves; that is, the generally deplorable working conditions these men had to endure. In the very moving book, *Death on the Ice,* Cassie Brown describes the hardships sealers were put through. Reportedly, ships were often overcrowded and filthy with bloody seal carcasses and fat sometimes serving as the men's beds. Traditionally the sealer supplied their own clothing and gear; not surprisingly, both of these were often inadequate. Reportedly, the food they were fed was usually insufficient to keep a body nourished under such harsh conditions. Sealers had to buy their berths on the larger vessels and it was not unusual, after a poor season, for a sealer to return from the voyage in debt. In addition to all these problems, sealing was an extremely dangerous occupation; sealers had to jump off moving vessels and coppy from one slippery ice pan to another. Injuries included frostbite and broken bones, among others. Many of you will be familiar with the story of the S.S. Newfoundland, the 1914 disaster in which seventy-seven sealers froze to death over a period of two days on the ice.

Why were these conditions allowed to persist? One reason was that there was always an abundant supply of sealers so firms like Bowring's and Harvey's were under no pressure to improve conditions on their ships. Even while the seal hunt was under attack, the difficulties the sealers faced did not become an issue. It is true that the crews of the 1970s and 80s did not have it as hard as the crew of the S.S. Greenland back around 1900 but they did not have it easy. Following this lecture is an excerpt from Guy Wright's *Sons and Seals: A Voyage to the Ice* which describes the long hours and gruelling labour the modern-day sealers endured.

In Newfoundland culture, hardship is glorified, perhaps because there is so much of it. Disasters on the ice, such as that of the S.S. Newfoundland, have become part of the province's folk culture. Survivors like Cecil Mouland became heroes. Going to the ice and sealing became a test of manhood. Captains like Abram Kean became awesome deities. This is one way a society copes with the things it cannot (or thinks it cannot) change; this is the way Newfoundland society has coped. Protest has been rare.

Other social scientists, such as Sinclair and Wright, have pointed to other, related aspects of sealing in Newfoundland Sinclair says:[33]

> In the rural communities of northern Newfoundland, an individual's personal reputation and social status depend on how well that person conforms to the predominant values of the community...Anyone who is seen to be working hard at the available opportunities in the area and making every effort to remain economically independent is generally respected, regardless of his/her current employment status.
>
> The seal hunt thus provides a major opportunity for men who have no other work options to demonstrate their commitment to an important cultural value of the community. Men who make every effort to pursue the seal hunt and who may relinquish their entitlement to unemployment insurance to do so are highly respected in these communities.

In addition, there is pride in the skills used in the longliner and land seal fisheries, as well as in the offshore hunt. And similar to many other cultures, hardiness and the ability to provide for one's family are two criteria of manhood.

Finally, sealing has become a symbol of Newfoundland culture; a unique symbol at that. This is very important—it helps

[33] Sinclair, p. 58.

explain why I and so many other Newfoundlanders at that time reacted so strongly to the attacks on the seal fishery. To us, they hit directly at our essence as members of this society and culture; they invalidated Newfoundland itself (and us) when they invalidated seal harvesting. This is why the counter-protest movements had names with overtones, sometimes blatant, sometimes subtle, of Newfoundland nationalism. Two examples that come to mind are "Young Newfoundlanders Fighting Back" and "Codpeace". The next lecture explores the process through which the historical off-shore seal hunt met its demise.

Sociological terms

Domestic commodity producers—those who produce goods (e.g., salmon, carrots) for use in their own province or country.

Economic spinoff—the economic activity that results indirectly from an enterprise or industry. (E.g., a spinoff sector of the fishery is fisheries-related manufacturing, such as producing boxes for fish or traps for lobster.)

Primary producers—farmers and fishermen/women, those who harvest natural resources for the consumption of others or for further processing.

Stereotype—a conventional expression of the character of a particular race, nationality or gender. The stereotyped person is portrayed as having no individuality. (E.g., Negroes are good dancers and athletes.)

Truck system—the non-cash, economic system whereby fishermen supplied merchants with fish in return for household and other provisions.

Lecture 7

The seal hunt protests

Setting the stage for protest

Although it is not well known, the seal hunt protests had their beginnings as early as 1920. Then and throughout the 1930s the concern was over the health of the herds; conservationists claimed numbers were declining so they wanted some regulations put in place. In 1950, just after Confederation, the Canadian government's Fisheries Research Board (FRB) carried out studies that showed that seals were being exploited to potentially dangerous levels. Following this, some controls on the hunt were established. Still, there were problems. Clearly, this was an industry run on an *ad hoc* basis with little regard for the seal herds or the people who culled them. Harold Horwood, a Newfoundland writer, and others pointed to the wastefulness in sealing; only the pelt and one flipper was taken while 80% of the meat was left to rot on the ice. While such practices were eventually legislated away, it was already too late to prevent the demise of the seal hunt. By the early 1960s the price of seal pelts was beginning to drop.

Protesting

The campaign to end the seal hunt was carefully managed; it was also slick, apparently well-funded and successful. Film makers brought the seal hunt into the international arena with scenes of hunters clubbing whitecoats and skinning seals, sometimes while they were alive. 1964 was the first year such films were released; film and photography became the backbone of the anti-sealing campaign. The International Fund for Animal Welfare (IFAW), for example, hired the advertising firm McCann-Erickson to direct a $100,000 "Stop the Seal Hunt" campaign in 1974. In time the anti-sealing forces became a *social movement*, or collective attempt to change some or all aspects of society. Later they would use petitioning, letter writing, demonstrating and even violence to achieve their goals. These are standard methods used by social movements in our society. More specifically, members of Greenpeace and the other protest groups used tactics that included dyeing seals green (so their pelts would be unmarketable), sitting on seals so that hunters couldn't club them, and, as I mentioned earlier in this unit, chaining themselves to the sealing vessels.

By 1983, the main consumer of seal pelts, the European Economic Community (EEC), had banned the importation of seal products, thus destroying the industry. EEC decision-makers were responding to public sentiment, especially in Britain and Germany, which by then was primarily against the hunt. Newfoundland's destiny has always been shaped by international forces, such as conflict between France and England, or the need for unskilled labour in the New England states; the destruction of the seal hunt fits into this pattern, as well. Although we tend to think of ourselves as an island, isolated and removed from the influence of the rest of the world, that perception is not an accurate one, either historically or in modern times.

The seal hunt today

The seal hunt is an economic, social and cultural institution that reaches far back into Newfoundland's history. We saw that it was important in the settlement patterns for the Northeast Coast of the island, for instance. Over time some social institutions will die out while others will *adapt*. My view is that the Newfoundland seal hunt did a little of both. The offshore seal hunt has been eliminated, to be sure, but some seal hunting still occurs. This takes place in two forms: the land-based hunts and the longliner hunt. Let's look briefly at these.

The longliner seal hunt begins in December and ends in late May, depending on location, of course, and ice conditions. Crews go out for a length of time varying between a day and a month; often, they will venture 100 miles offshore. There are usually three to six in the crew, depending largely on the size of the vessel. Longliner crews normally shoot seals, using high-powered rifles, while they are in the water or on pans of ice. In their report Sinclair et al. emphasized that seal harvesting is an integral part of the seasonal round of economic activities for longliner operations in northern Newfoundland. This has only increased as the cost of operating a longliner and repaying loans has gone up.

Although there isn't time or space here to study the economic impact of declining (and disappearing) sealing revenues, one example pertaining to the longliner hunt will illustrate that this is significant:[34]

> The impact of the loss of sealing revenues is clearly evident in the Marine Services Centres along the northeast coast. In 1985, as late as the middle of May, longliners were still hauled up and little activity was evident in preparation for the fishery. In former years, these centres would have been a hive of activity as fishermen worked on their vessels making repairs, checking engines and gear and waiting for the ice to clear in order to begin the fishery. The loss of sealing income means that in order to prepare for the fishery, owner-operators will either have to obtain credit, thereby increasing their indebtedness, or begin fishing without making essential repairs or obtaining new gear.

The "landsmen" are the largest group of sealers (there were 4989 licensed in 1982, including Labrador). But not all license holders participate in seal harvesting; in fact, the degree of participation varies considerably. This hunt may or may not be commercial—that is, very often seal products are harvested exclusively for household use. Even in cases where seals are harvested for commercial purposes, the money earned is nominal. Still, even a small amount of

---

[34] Sinclair et al, 1989, p. 46.

money is appreciated in rural Newfoundland where there are limited opportunities to earn cash. Landsmen go out in their speedboats each day and shoot seals on ice or in the water. In many ways, this form of sealing is a modern adaptation of the way our aboriginal forebears used to hunt seals, in small open boats using spears of various sorts. In the early 1990s, there is some talk of sealing making a comeback; certainly seal fur coats are becoming increasingly popular among urban, middle class Newfoundlanders. It will be interesting to watch the adaptations the sealing industry makes in the future, particularly in terms of public relations and international marketing. It appears highly improbable that the 'glory days' of the fleet will ever return and, as so many times before, Newfoundland society will make its adjustments.

Sociological term

Social movement—a collective attempt to reform some or all aspects of society.

Reading

(excerpts from)

A day on the ice

by Guy Wright

Morning (p. 55)

"Come on boys, all hands out of the bunks now, breakfast'll soon be ready," the mate called at ten minutes to four.

Every part of my body ached as I turned over in the narrow bunk, fooling myself that I could ignore the wake-up call. This was our second morning at the ice. The day before had been a long battle against wind, rain and slippery ice. When we had finally got to bed at 1 a.m., I was so exhausted I had trouble falling asleep.

Norman rolled out of his bunk and lit a cigarette. He was fully dressed except for his outside clothing. He pulled his rubber boots over two pairs of wool socks and stumbled out the door. I could hear him urinate into the drain at the rail.

By the time I got myself on deck most of the crew were already

---

busy stowing the pelts that had been left on deck to chill overnight. We had taken nearly a thousand pelts the first day and about 400 were still on the deck. Each man took two pelts from the neat piles by the rail, carried them to the hatch, and tossed them into the hold, where other men caught them and stacked them within the pounds. It was a good way to limber up in the morning, but I wished we had been given more than three hours' sleep.

Weather-wise, it promised to be a reasonably good day. It was below freezing, and the wind, which had gusted to 95 kilometers an hour the first day, had died down.

(p. 56)

It is a tricky maneuver to jump from a moving ship to a slab of ice, especially when carrying unwieldy flagpoles and hakkapiks. Occasionally a man falls into the water. This is a particularly dangerous predicament, since a moving ship is not easy to handle in a delicate situation and the man can be crushed if the captain is not adept with the wheel. In 1980 a man on a different vessel was killed when he slipped between the ship and a piece of ice while trying to climb aboard. The swell forced him under. It was the first fatal accident at the hunt for many years. Although this incident was tragic, it points out the modern industry's generally excellent safety record, despite the ever-present dangers.

Killing
(p. 57)

Killing a seal pup is physically an easy task. One sharp blow to its head with the hammer end of the hakkapik usually smashes the small, fragile skull, causing massive haemorrhaging to the brain. Although nervous reflex action often causes the body to move in a sort of swimming motion, sometimes mistaken for the seal's still being alive, it is almost certainly dead or irreversibly unconscious with the first blow. But it is hit twice more to be certain. If the sealer thinks the animal might still be alive, he touches the eyeball, and if it blinks he strikes it again until this reflex disappears.

(pp. 57–58)

Billy bravely laughed off the teasing he got about having enough nerve to kill his first seal, but when the time came he could scarcely bring himself to do the job. He managed to kill and pelt only two seals the first day, and was reported to the captain by his master watch for not working hard enough. The captain understood the problem and told Billy to help the others towing pelts to the collecting pan until he got used to clubbing seals. The next day Billy was able to brace himself for a larger kill.

Some of the other green hands later said they too were nervous about killing their first few seals. The captain's sympathetic response to Billy makes me think it is a common experience. Billy's reaction may have been more extreme, but it was understandable given his inexperience and youth. The sheer number of seals killed, combined with the strenuous and dangerous nature of the work, help the sealer from becoming absorbed in moral or emotional questions about the slaughter.

(p. 58)

Skinning or "pelting" a seal is more unnerving. It brings one into a direct and personal contact with the animal. Once dead, the pup's pelt is cut in a smooth stroke from the chin to the tip of its small tail. One feels warm life-giving blood turn cold on one's hand and face. (The seal's body holds a great amount of blood, necessary to keep it alive in such a cold climate.) For a practiced hand the job takes about three minutes. The fat-laden pelt separates easily from the carcass, but one must be careful not to tear the pelt when trimming the face and head. The form left on the ice is lifeless and cold. It is not a pleasant experience, but when the act is repeated 10,000 times over a period of ten days, the sealer soon adjusts to his work.

(pp. 59–60)

After the trip was over, several of the men complained about those who had done poor jobs of pelting and had reduced the value of the shares. This disapproval was not expressed during the trip because it would have been demeaning to a crew member when everyone was presumably doing his best. Since it was not customary to give extra lessons, tolerance was the only alternative.

Yet, if a man was clearly not trying to do his share, he would be ostracized by his fellows, and perhaps reported to the captain. Billy experienced both. When the men thought he was not working hard enough, Billy was given the "cold shoulder" by the experienced men whom he most wanted to impress. To show their disappointment they became coldly polite and joked with him less. This treatment lasted a day, until Billy proved himself capable and, more importantly, willing to work like any of them.

The previous year a sealer did not live up to the others' expectations, and he was thought to have tainted the whole voyage. "We had a pretty good trip last year, but it could have been better; we had one guy that didn't pull his weight and that sort of spoils things," the chief engineer told me.

Tolerance of mild incompetence and intolerance of laziness reflect the fraternal feelings of solidarity among the crew. Sloppy pelting can result in lost wages for everyone; but if an inexperienced man is trying to do his share and still cannot match the abilities of others, he is not faulted. A man who is attempting to do his job is confirming that he sees himself as a regular part of the crew. A man who neglects his share of the work is breaking a trust with his fellow workers and placing an extra burden on them.

Freezing (pp. 66–68)

I soon found I could not do even the easiest work. I sat near the pan with several men who were smoking cigarettes, trying to shield themselves from the freezing wind behind a ridge of ice. My feet were past the painful stage—they were numb. But I thought there were still some circulation in them. My legs were cold and I cursed myself for not putting on the oilskins, even if they were wet. At least they would have cut the wind. My hands were useless because I could not put them into the fingers of my frozen gloves, and to work without gloves seemed foolish, despite Isaac's advice.

The men I sat with did not say much. One muttered that we should go back to the ship, since it was close now and we were not accomplishing much anyway. But he was not a master watch, and we remembered the captain's admonition the previous day: "Don't go back to the ship unless told to do so." Soon they got up and tried to do more work, to keep warm more than anything else. I saw that the third watch was not far away, and they seemed to be huddled together and not working. I thought I might as well have company if I could not work, so I announced I was going to join them.

Most of this watch stood with their backs to the wind, slapping their arms across their chests to keep the circulation going. Ches, the master watch, kept busy killing seals and hauling them around to the pan. With each two he brought over, he would urge his men to keep working. "That's the best way to stay warm." But few of the men heeded his advice. Everyone was too cold and tired to work.

When the seals were split open, the men thrust their hands into the steaming blood, desperately seeking warmth. When the blood started to cool, someone cut away more of the fat and men stood on the pelt sapping the last bit of warmth from the dead pup. It was a macabre sight, but the only practical thing to do in such a situation. By now the ship had moved away by a kilometer, but the men thought it would soon return to pick them up. It was about 5:30 p.m.—an hour left to wait.

Soon James' watch came over to join us. Fourteen men huddled against the wind, mucous and condensation frozen to their moustaches. One young man had only three shirts for protection; he rubbed snow on his face where frostbite had started to turn the skin white. My feet felt like wood but I was not sure whether they were frozen or just numb.

An hour can be an eternity. We felt certain the captain would turn the ship around and come and get us. Surely he must realize we were not working. Ches kept busy hauling seals to us, and he still tried to convince the men they, too, should work to stay warm, but he convinced no one.[35]

---

[35] The captain was in fact worried that we were not working. But the ship was stuck, and his megaphone would not carry far enough to reach us, and so he had no way of telling us to

Someone said that it must have been like this in the old days, referring to the many times men froze to death on the ice, but particularly to the grotesque disaster of 1914. We were getting a taste of the same situation. A fine day had suddenly turned bitter, catching us unprepared.

At six o'clock, some of the men suggested walking to the ship. I tried to argue against them because I knew I would not be able to keep up and did not relish being left behind. But when it became obvious that the ship was stuck in the ice, we had little choice but to strike off. The master watches agreed and we walked off in single file.

(p. 70)

If the work lasted more than a few hours (which it normally did), the evening became the hardest part of the day. The work was easier and the ship provided warmth when needed, but the men craved sleep, their legs ached and their fingers were numb. Muscles began to stiffen from the day's exertions. The captain could not see who was on deck, and enough men were milling about so that one less would probably not be noticed except by a few. But the men took pride in the ability to work well for long hours under adverse conditions.

After the hunt, Billy told me had had chafed himself so badly that he bled through his pants. He applied some first-aid cream, then dressed and went back on deck, even though his master watch had told him to stay in his bunk. "It got better," he said, "and I'm glad now that I did it. It feels good to remember things like that." During the first day on the ice, one man had fallen and cracked a rib. He kept working on deck that night until he stiffened in the cold and the pain became too much to bear. He received some first aid from the chief engineer and went back to help sharpen knives. The work did not end until one in the morning.

---

come to the ship.

References for Unit 4

- Mr. Craig Allen, interview with. Department of Labour, Government of Newfoundland and Labrador, June 10, 1991.
- Raoul Andersen. "Nineteenth Century American Banks Fishing Under Sail: Its Health and Injury Costs'. In *Canadian Folklore*, Vol. 12 (2), 1990, p. 85-122, Laval, Montreal. Also published in *Maritime Identity, Canadian Folklore*, Volume 12, Number 2, 1990, The Folklore Studies Association of Canada, Québec.
- Cassie Brown with Harold Horwood. *Death on the Ice*, Doubleday, 1972.
- E. Calvin Coish. *Season of the Seal: The International Storm Over Canada's Seal Hunt*, Breakwater, 1979.
- Parcival Copes. "Community Resettlement and Rationalization of the Fishing Industry in Newfoundland," a paper presented to the Canadian Economics Association, June, 1971, in *The Political Economy of Newfoundland, 1929–1972*, Peter Neary (ed.) Copp Clark, Toronto, 1973, pp. 226–232.
- John Kenneth Galbraith. *The Nature of Mass Poverty*, Penguin, 1979.
- Wyn Grant. *The Political Economy of Industrial Policy*, Butterworth & Co. Ltd., London, 1982.
- Maura Hanrahan. "Living on the Dead: The UI System for Fishermen," Institute of Social & Economic Research. MUN, St. John's, 1988.
- Maura Hanrahan. " 'We Won't Even Get a Sculpin': The Conflict Between Traditional Economic Adaptations in Newfoundland and Federal Government Fisheries Policy." M.A. Thesis, 1986.

- Maura Hanrahan. "Government Action in Troubled Industry: The Restructuring of Newfoundland's Industrial Fisheries in the Early 1980s," Ph.D. thesis, 1989.
- Arthur J. Hanson and Cynthia Lamson. "Fisheries Decision-Making in Atlantic Canada: Problems and Prospects," in Lamson and Hanson (eds.), 1984, pp. 235–241.
- Robert H. Hill. *The Meaning of Work and the Reality of Unemployment in the Newfoundland Context,* Community Services Council, Newfoundland & Labrador, February, 1983.
- Stuart Holland. *The Regional Problem,* The Macmillan Press Ltd., London, 1976.
- Douglas House, Chair. *Building on our Strengths: Report of the Royal Commission on Employment and Unemployment,* Government of Newfoundland & Labrador, 1986.
- Gordon Inglis. *More Than Just a Union: The Story of the FFAWU,* Jesperson, 1985.
- Noel Iverson & D. Ralph Matthews. *Communities in Decline: An Examination of Household Resettlement in Newfoundland,* ISER, St. John's, 1968.
- Otto Kelland. *Dories and Dorymen,* Robinson-Blackmore, St. John's, 1984.
- Gordon Laxer, ed. *Perspectives on Canadian Economic Development: Class, Staples, Gender, and Elites,* Oxford University Press, Toronto, 1991.
- Elliott Leyton. *Dying Hard: The Ravages of Industrial Carnage,* McClelland & Stewart, Toronto, 1975.
- David Macdonald. "Power Begins at the Cod End": The Newfoundland Trawlermen's Strike, 1974-75, ISER, St. John's, 1980.
- Ralph Matthews. *The Creation of Regional Dependency.* University of Toronto Press, Toronto, 1983.

- Malcolm Moseley. *Growth Centres in Spatial Planning,* Pergammon Press Ltd., Oxford, 1974.
- Harry W. Richardson. *Elements of Regional Economics,* Penguin, Harmondsworth, Middlesex, UK, 1969.
- Harry W. Richardson. *Regional and Urban Economics,* Pitman, London, 1979.
- Frederick Rowe. *A History of Newfoundland & Labrador,* Toronto, McGraw-Hill Ryerson, 1980.
- Donald Savoie. *Regional Economic Development: Canada's Search for Solutions,* University of Toronto Press, Toronto, 1984.
- Peter Sinclair. *From Traps to Draggers: Domestic Commodity Production in Northwest Newfoundland, 1850-1982.* ISER, St. John's, 1985.
- Peter Sinclair. *State Intervention in the Newfoundland Fisheries,* Avebury, Aldershot, U.K., 1987.
- Peter R. Sinclair, Robert H. Hill, Cynthia Lamson and H.A. Williamson. *Social and Cultural Aspects of Sealing in Atlantic Canada,* ISER, Report No. 5, September, 1989.
- Guy David Wright. *Sons & Seals: A Voyage to the Ice,* ISER, 1984.